Updating and Enhancing Course Content, Course Delivery, and Academic Management

Angus Hooke and Greg Whateley

Table of Contents

Foreword

This book, a follow-on to *Transitioning to Online Learning During COVID-19: Reflections by Practitioners,* continues the stories of the lecturers, technology specialists, and management staff at UBSS as they move deeper into the new academic world of online and blended learning. The direct changes facing UBSS are occurring while the industries and disciplines covered by its academic courses are experiencing unprecedented change. This book focuses on how academics have incorporated changes that are taking place in the business world into the content of their courses and how they have adopted and adapted online tools to make their lessons more engaging for students. It also discusses how senior management is addressing topics of increasing importance such as the growth of online program management (OPM) companies and assessing teaching performance in an online environment. The lessons and suggestions made by our practitioners will be of great help to other UBSS staff and management. However, the information contained in the 18 chapters of this book should also provide interesting reading and practical ideas to other stakeholders in the higher education sector.

Alan Manly, OAM

Chairman and CEO

Group Colleges Australia

Preface

In early 2020, when the COVID-19 pandemic required higher education providers to move abruptly from onsite to offsite learning, the prevailing attitude among students and academics was one of concern about the quality of the education that would be provided in the new environment. As small problems such as how to keep current courses on track were solved and more difficult challenges such as maintaining student, staff and institutional viability were largely being met, both students and providers began to feel more confident with online learning and switched attention, slowly and cautiously at first, to the new and interesting opportunities that online technologies were offering. Many students realised that online learning, when properly delivered, can be engaging and can produce considerable savings in both time and money. Some providers realised that a superior product could be made available at a lower cost per student by having appropriately trained academics deliver classes from campus in purpose-designed studios, with each student having the choice of accessing them either face-to-face or online. Universities were encouraged to consider the option of greater specialisation in their main area of comparative education - research and training researchers – by outsourcing part or all course-based teaching to the new online program management companies.

Within a period of about 18 months, higher education moved from complacently delivering education face-to-face using in-house resources to more confidently exploring the new opportunities that the pandemic had forced to the surface. Academics realised that the accelerating pace of change in their own business environment was being mirrored in the business fields they taught, and these required ongoing changes to the content of the academic courses related to those fields. They also realised that rapidly changing technologies were offering new and generally more engaging and effective ways of delivering course content. In addition, managers became aware that technological developments were providing more efficient tools for structuring and operating their businesses and business units. This book describes the experiences of lecturers and managers at a leading higher education provider, Universal Business School Sydney (UBSS) as they worked through this challenging but also exciting transition period to a new normal in higher education.

SECTION 1: COURSE CONTENT

Advances in digital technology require business students to work with larger and different forms of data and to learn new methods of detecting patterns and key associations hidden in these data. The authors of Chapter 1 discuss three new algorithms that they believe students should study, namely, the apriori, the k-means, and the C4.5 classifier algorithms to identify these patterns and associations. They make a compelling case for including these algorithms in curricula for quantitative methods, explain each algorithm, and discuss their key applications. The authors argue that understanding the algorithms will equip business students with better skills and greater knowledge for success in the modern business environment.

Since the advent of the Digital Era, marketing departments have been placing increasing reliance on information and technologies from rapidly developing fields such as neuroscience and artificial intelligence as well as on social media to develop their marketing strategies. The authors of Chapter 2 point out that marketing education has not kept pace with these changes, and that the gap between marketing practice and marketing education has been widening. They suggest that this trend can be reversed by adding three new topics to traditional marketing curricula, namely, neuromarketing, humanistic marketing, and artificial intelligence.

The author of Chapter 3 both heads a Centre for Entrepreneurship and teaches postgraduate students how to prepare entrepreneurship and business reports. In this chapter, he points out that the growth of new e-commerce sales and marketing platforms and tools such as data-driven marketing, voice search engines, and Afterpay, along with the growing incidence of major shocks like COVID-19, have substantially changed the environment in which new businesses start and operate. He explains, with real-life examples, how he has changed the content and delivery of a postgraduate subject to accommodate these changes.

Academics are continually updating their courses to reflect changes in the content (structure and behaviour) of their discipline, the understanding by the academic community of this content, and the content needs of the students who are enrolled in the course. In Chapter 4, two authors who teach an undergraduate course in Economics at a higher education institution in Sydney discuss the increasing importance of technological unemployment, and how they have changed the content of their course to accommodate this development.

COVID 19 has changed consumer behaviour and buying patterns. As a result, marketers need to find new ways to reach out to consumers and get them to buy their products. The author Chapter 5 suggests that the 4Ps approach – Product, Price, Place, and Promotion – that was developed by Philip Kotler, is still relevant in marketing but the description and meaning of some of the Ps have changed. During the pandemic, the 4Ps have morphed into Product, Price, People and Process. Marketers now grappling with the People and Process components, and academics must ensure that students are properly trained to meet this new focus of marketing practice, especially the Process component.

Throughout the Industrial Era (1800-2000), a major concern of economists was the conflict between the effects of continuing increases in population and income on the demand for food and the finite supply of arable land on the supply of food. Traditional courses in Resource Economics highlighted the Malthusian model that preached abstinence and frugality but predicted famines and early deaths. However, since the 1960s the growth rate of population has declined, per capita consumption of food has reached saturation point for about 40% of the global population, and new technologies have led to excess supply and falling real prices in farm product markets, increasing poverty among farmers, and withdrawal of land from the farming sector. In Chapter 6, the authors discuss the outlook for the farm products market during the remainder of the 21st century. They also show how recent projections have been incorporated into an undergraduate course in Economics at a higher education provider in Sydney.

SECTION 2: COURSE DELIVERY

The invention and development of computing hardware and accounting software have transformed accounting practices. Processes that were performed manually in the latter part of the 20th century are now executed by computers using sophisticated accounting software packages. As a result, new graduates entering the accounting profession must not only possess a thorough knowledge of accounting principles and processes, they must also have strong computing skills. The author of Chapter 7 discusses how she introduced a sophisticated computer package into a postgraduate course in accounting and how combining this with an appropriate weight in assessments increased student motivation, participation, and performance.

Achieving the engagement of learners is a challenging task. The challenge is especially daunting when lessons are delivered online. Devising mitigating strategies requires a clear understanding of the ground realities. Chapter 8 explores these and other issues concerning learner engagement. Since the onset of the COVID-19 pandemic and the switch to online learning, international students in non-university settings appear to have been less engaged for various reasons, and some of those reasons seem easier to manage than others. To prevent the effectiveness and sustainability of academic programs from being unintended casualties of the move to online learning, complacency should not be an option.

For many years educators have sought to integrate videos into their pedagogical practices. To support 'blended learning - a thoughtful fusion of face-to-face and online learning experiences' (Garrison & Vaughn, 2008), the author of Chapter 9 developed a package of five-minute videos (called 'vodcasts') and used them in a postgraduate economics subject. The vodcasts were designed to introduce key economic concepts to students as a precursor and complement to face-to-face teaching. They were intended to be a flexible resource that addressed student diversity and helped students transition from undergraduate to postgraduate study. In this chapter, he discusses the evolution of the project and the effects on student learning. Surveys and focus groups indicate that student perceptions of the vodcasts were resoundingly positive.

The traditional mode of delivering tertiary education has focused on face-to-face classes delivered to increasingly diverse global student cohorts. COVID-19 forced most providers to move abruptly to online delivery and, in countries exporting education, to smaller cohorts as international borders were closed. The author of Chapter 10 argues that online delivery is here to stay, and that providers can learn from marketers how to make their product more attractive to students in order succeed in a more competitive education environment.

The digital workplace is the main driver of the recent changes in business communication. It has also significantly altered the content and delivery methods of teaching and learning. Interactions with students now require a new set of cognitive and physical skills. Chapter 11 contains an analysis of the types of technical tools, applications, and elements of business communication within the digital workplace and their effects on the scholarship of students, on lecturers, and on educational institutions.

Surveys conducted in three major Latin American (LATAM) countries in early 2020 showed that COVID-19 has created considerable uncertainty for students. However, they also showed that the sector has the capacity to make positive, permanent changes, and that institutions that are flexible and able to adapt quickly are most likely to succeed in the new and changed environment. The author of Chapter 12 discusses how institutional flexibility at UBSS allowed him to introduce a new digital tool in an accounting subject and analyses the effect this change had on student satisfaction and acquisition of key employability skills.

SECTION 3: ACADEMIC MANAGEMENT

The COVID-19 pandemic produced an involuntary shift to online learning – in its many manifestations. In turn, this highlighted and facilitated a range of alternative modes of delivery for international students. These are sometimes referred to as flexible modes of delivery and at other times as alternative modes of delivery. The traditional face-to-face mode has been overtaken (certainly for a period) by a range of alternative arrangements that cater for lockdowns and community restrictions. The author of Chapter 13 argues that the most challenging part of these restrictions was their unpredictability, which made planning and strategy difficult. He notes that the option of having alternatives to face-to-face delivery ready and available has become a highly valued commodity.

As with many other industries, higher education is filled with Three Letter Acronyms (TLA), such as CRM, SMS, SIS, LMS and FTE. However, Online Program Management (OPM) is not just another TLA. Rather, OPM has the potential to totally change how unit content is developed, the way and by whom it is delivered, the student experience, and the business models that manage these. In Chapter 14, the author outlines current developments in OPM and presents four scenarios on how OPMs will change higher education during the 2020s.

The COVID-19 pandemic has forced the higher education sector in Australia to move from mainly face-to-face to wholly online delivery. Thea author of Chapter 15 uses her own experience as a lecturer at three different institutions to highlight the variety of ways in which the sector has managed the transition, including the provision of support for lecturers – good and bad - and the use of student feedback on the effectiveness of teaching.

The use of SETs for evaluating instructors and courses is a controversial, sometimes political, and often hotly debated issue in many college and university staffrooms. Some instructors and administrators argue that the information provided by SET ratings and comments helps them perform their roles more effectively, while others (mainly instructors) maintain that the instrument has biases and other weaknesses that make its use counterproductive. The effectiveness of the instrument also depends on the participation rate, which appears to be substantially lower for online learning. Chapter 16 discusses the advantages and disadvantages of SETs and makes suggestions on how they can best be used in both face-to-face and online learning environments.

Knowledge and intellectual capital are key resources driving the knowledge economy. Organisations are seeking to gain a competitive advantage and improve their business performance by increasing their knowledge and enhancing their intellectual capabilities in an ever-changing business environment. However, how to effectively utilise and leverage knowledge and intellectual capital to maximise organisational value is a constant challenge for management. The author of Chapter 17 reviews and discusses the dimensions of intellectual capital, the key components of the knowledge management system, the dynamic interactions among these, and the roles they play in creating value within organisations.

Support for the view that the primary objective of companies should be to maximise the wealth of shareholders is based on the Adam Smith principle that the best way for a person to promote the social interest is to pursue their self-interest. However, companies are increasingly being asked to add a range of secondary objectives, mainly concerned with diversity, equity, and the environment. Some proponents of the broader approach maintain that they are not challenging the traditional business model, and that the secondary objectives are effectively mediating variables that facilitate the maximisation of profits and shareholder wealth. The authors of Chapter 18 develop a model to facilitate analysis of some of the effects of one secondary objective – greater diversity – on economic welfare. They also consider how one education provider in Sydney has addressed the challenge of achieving optimum diversity among its students.

Section 1:

Course Content

Chapter

1

Teaching Quantitative Methods: A Look into the Future

Arash Najmaei, Independent Consultant

Zahra Sadeghinejad, Universal Business School Sydney

ABSTRACT

Advances in digital technology require business students to work with larger and different forms of data and to learn new methods of detecting patterns and key associations hidden in these data. This chapter discusses three new algorithms that the authors believe students should study, namely, the apriori, the k-means, and the C4.5 classifier algorithms. They make a strong case for including these algorithms in curricula for quantitative methods, explain each algorithm, and discuss some of their applications. The authors argue that understanding the algorithms will equip business students with better skills and greater knowledge for success in the modern business environment.

INTRODUCTION

The advent of Big Data Analytics and associated technologies such as Robotics, Internet of Things, Artificial Intelligence, Machine Learning, Deep Learning, and Cognitive Computing, have upended the traditional syllabus for teaching quantitative methods to business students (Vowels & Goldberg, 2019). Advances in business intelligence and analytics require business students to learn new statistical methods that are fundamentally different from traditional business statistics in two main ways: (1) they are not concerned with significance testing via p-value assessments, but focus on detecting new patterns and key associations hidden in big data (Simsek, Vaara, Paruchuri, Nadkarni, & Shaw, 2019); and (2) they are designed to work with new kinds of data, known as big data, which are different from typical quantitative data in both form and structure (George, Haas, & Pentland, 2014).

In this chapter, the authors discuss three algorithms: (1) the apriori algorithm, (2) the k-means algorithm, and (3) the C4.5 classifier algorithm, all of which are widely used in big data analytics across industries (Wu et al., 2007). First, they make a case for including these algorithms in the curriculum for quantitative methods. Then, they elaborate on each algorithm and explain some of their applications. The authors argue that including these algorithms in quantitative methods subjects will equip business students with much-needed skills and knowledge for success in today's changing industries, where a major key to success is an understanding and appreciation of knowledge about big data and advanced analytics.

WHY SHOULD WE TEACH NEW ALGORITHMS?

The business world has entered the era of Analytics 3.0, where access to big data and the use of advanced analytics are imperative to the everyday operation of large and small firms alike (Davenport, 2018). Business schools have the crucial responsibility of equipping business students with the mindset and skills required for success in this era. As eloquently argued by Simon (1967):

> *"The tasks of a business school are to train men for the practice of management (or some special branch of management) as a profession, and to develop new knowledge that may be relevant to improving the operation of business" (p.1).*

To this end, the authors call for a new curriculum for quantitative methods. Their proposed curriculum emphasizes analytical algorithms that are part of the movement toward Analytics 3.0. The full list of algorithms in big data analytics (see Brownlee, 2017) goes beyond the scope of this chapter. In what follows the authors describe three such algorithms, selected because of their popularity, applicability, and more importantly their complementarity (Wu et al., 2007).

C4.5 CLASSIFIER ALGORITHM

Description

C4.5 is a classifier, or decision-making tree, algorithm within the class of machine-learning techniques. It was developed by Quinlan (1993) as an improvement on the ID3 algorithm (Quinlan, 1979). In simple terms, C4.5 looks at a large set of items - such as customers, transactions, and purchases - in a dataset and develops an initial tree assuming similarity between all items. It then uses a divide-and-conquer logic to find branches between items by grouping them into smaller sets using a statistical test. C4.5 employs two heuristics to achieve this: (1) information gain, which minimizes the total entropy of the subsets; and (2) the default gain ratio, which divides information gain by the information provided in the test outcomes (Wu et al., 2007).

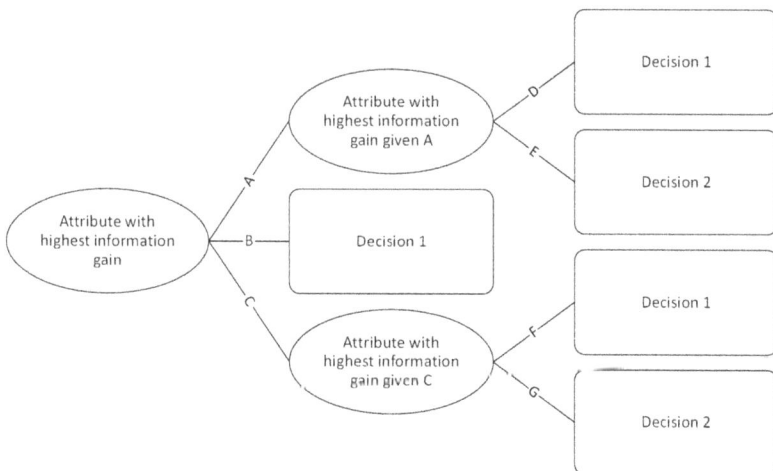

Figure 1 - A sample decision tree generated by c4.5 algorithm[1]

---

[1] *https://www.quora.com/What-is-the-C4-5-algorithm-and-how-does-it-work*

The initial tree is then pruned to avoid overfitting. Research on C4.5 was funded for many years by the Australian Research Council and is freely available for research and teaching[2].

Some business applications

The C4.5 algorithm has wide applications across industries. Its robustness, accuracy, and theoretical rigour allow it to be applied to a wide range of data sets. For instance, marketers can use decision trees to determine the demographics of shoppers who choose a retailer or buy a specific product range. They can use shopper panel data to determine the best age ranges of shoppers, then dig further into the income ranges in each age range, and even go further into how the choice of retailers is explained by each income range within each age range. The findings of such decision trees can help managers decide on distributions, promotions, and advertising strategies. Similarly, finance professionals can use C4.5 to develop decision trees that explain how credit cards, insurance premiums, and loan applications can be distributed to customers in terms of their occupations, demographics, and locations.

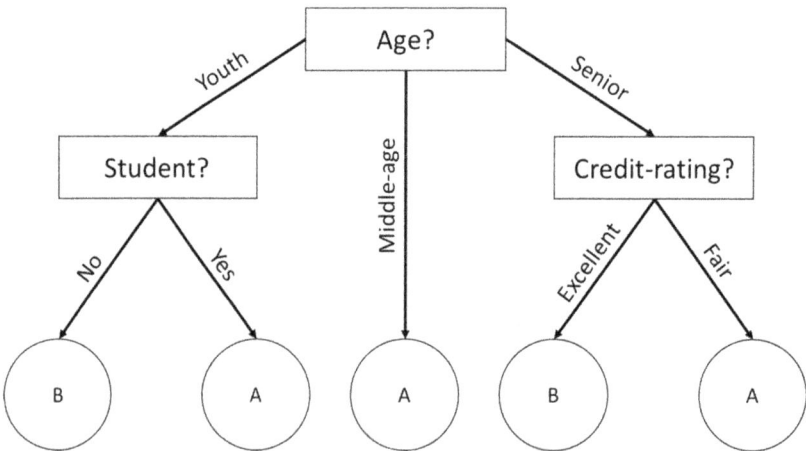

Figure 2 - a Decision tree generated by C4.5 algorithm for a sample of mobile users[3]

[2] https://sourceforge.net/directory/os:windows/?q=c4.5+algorithm
[3] https://europepmc.org/article/med/24688389

APRIORI ALGORITHM

Description

An apriori algorithm, also known as associate mining or affinity analysis, is a machine-learning tool to find itemset or explore associations between different items in a large population of transactions (Aguinis, Forcum, & Joo, 2012). It is characterized as a level-wise, complete-search algorithm which assumes that if an itemset is not frequent, none of its superset is ever frequent (Wu et al., 2007). It therefore allows researchers to identify those items that co-occur (i.e., appear together) on a frequent basis and to assess the extent to which they co-occur (Aguinis et al., 2012). The algorithm first searches for frequent occurrences. Once frequent item sets are obtained, it generates association rules with confidence larger than or equal to a user-specified minimum confidence level. Wu et al. (2007) explain the algorithm as follows:

> "Apriori first scans the database and searches for frequent item sets of size 1 by accumulating the count for each item and collecting those that satisfy the minimum support requirement. It then iterates on the following three steps and extracts all the frequent item sets. (1) Generate $Ck+1$, candidates of frequent itemsets of size $k + 1$, from the frequent item sets of size k. (2) Scan the database and calculate the support of each candidate of frequent item sets. (3) Add those item sets that satisfies the minimum support requirement to $Fk+1$." (P. 12-13).

Apriori algorithms, therefore, not only can explore, mine, and discover new relationships between various attributes in a dataset but also can be used to test hypotheses about expected relationships and co-occurrences. Three complementary metrics reveal the presence, nature, and strength of an association rule: lift, support, and confidence (Aguinis et al., 2012). Lift provides information on whether an association exists as well as whether the association is positive or negative. Support shows the probability that a set of items co-occurs with another set of items in a data set. Confidence reveals the probability that a set of items occurs given that another set of items has already occurred (Aguinis et al., 2012). The algorithm is quite simple, and the metrics are easy to compute.

Experimenting with apriori-like algorithms is the first thing that data miners try to do (Wu et al., 2007).

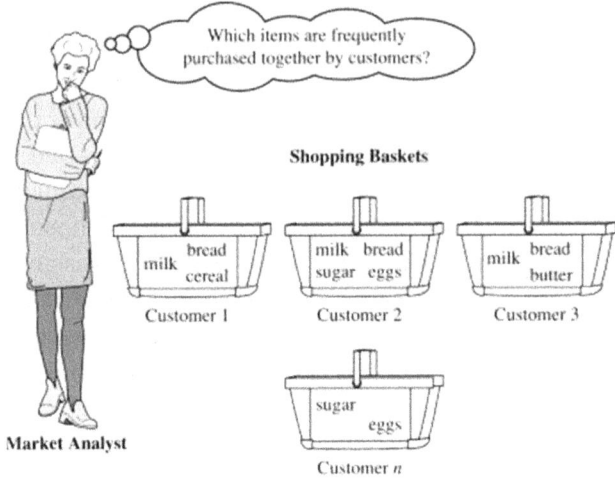

Figure 3 - An illustration of a fundamental business question that can be addressed by an Apriori algorithm[4]

Some business applications

There are many areas of business and management practice that can benefit from the use of apriori algorithms. For instance, HR managers can use employees' records to identify conditions that occur together when employees show a high degree of turnover, unexcused absenteeism, aggregation, or loss of motivation and work engagement. Similarly, marketing managers can employ this algorithm to mine associations between products that are purchased together, websites that are visited together, and consumer attributes that exist when certain shopper behaviours occur together. Leadership scholars and practitioners can also benefit from this algorithm by exploring leaders' attributes, behaviours, and skills that occur together under different conditions and in different contexts. For instance, apriori algorithms can be used to find associations between observable attributes of leaders who succeeded during the COVID-19 pandemic. Lastly, entrepreneurship researchers can utilise this

---

[4] *https://www.sciencedirect.com/topics/computer-science/market-basket-analysis*

algorithm to find a set of characteristics that occur together in successful or unsuccessful entrepreneurs or a set of skills that entrepreneurs demonstrate when raising funds. Aguinis et al. (2012) provide a more complete list of areas where management practitioners can benefit from this algorithm.

THE K-MEANS ALGORITHM

Description

The k-means algorithm is a simple yet very effective clustering algorithm. It is essentially an iterative method to partition a given dataset into a user-specified number of clusters, k. (Wu et al., 2007). The algorithm starts by picking k points in a dataset and their representative or closest centroids. Then the algorithm iterates between two steps till convergence (Wu et al., 2007):

1. Data Assignment. Each data point is assigned to its closest centroid, with ties broken arbitrarily. This results in a partitioning of the data.
2. Relocation of "means". Each cluster representative is relocated to the centre (mean) of all data points assigned to it.

The result of this iterative procedure is a set (k) of clearly defined groups for further analysis and informed decision making.

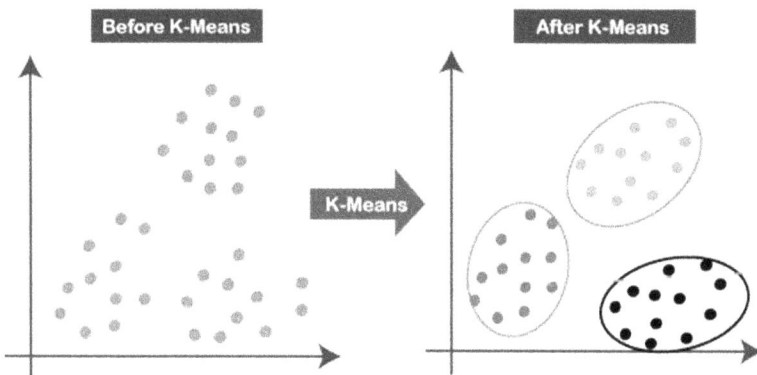

Figure 4 - An illustration of KNN algorithm[5]

---

[5] *https://www.analyticsvidhya.com/blog/2021/04/k-means-clustering-simplified-in-python/*

K-means algorithm is computationally fast, simple, and very effective, making it a widely used method for segmentation, clustering, and grouping purposes.

Some business applications

A k-means algorithm is a powerful clustering algorithm. It can be used by marketing practitioners to find market segments, as well as to target markets and product groups. More importantly, the simplicity of the algorithm allows marketing managers to apply it to any set of data, such as data from online transactions and social media campaigns, to explore how target audiences, prospect shoppers, and existing or loyal shoppers can be grouped so as to tailor marketing offerings to their specific wants and needs. Similarly, banks can use the algorithm to find optional groups of customers in terms of their credit scores and other attributes. Lastly, operations and supply-chain research can benefit from the algorithm in ways such as grouping of suppliers in terms of their contractual obligations, delays, errors, and powers or grouping of produce defaults and defects in terms of the types and levels of damage. The results enable managers to formulate different courses of actions for each cluster, which in turn improves the effectiveness and efficiency of operations.

CONCLUDING REMARKS

In this chapter, the authors illustrated how three algorithms from the field of machine learning and big data analytics can provide business students with a set of analytical skills that are essential in todays' data-driven job markets. It serves as a starting point for including more advanced analytics in the syllabus of business statistics and quantitative methods in order to train students to make better decisions and tackle more sophisticated business problems using more advanced analytical tools.

REFERENCES

Aguinis, H., Forcum, L. E., & Joo, H. (2012). *Using Market Basket Analysis in Management Research.* Journal of Management. doi:10.1177/0149206312466147.

Brownlee, J. (2017). *Master Machine Learning Algorithms: Discover How They Work and Implement Them From Scratch.* Melbourne, Australia: Mastery Machine Learning Series.

Davenport, T. H. (2018). *From analytics to artificial intelligence.* Journal of Business Analytics, 1(2), 73-80. doi:10.1080/2573234x.2018.1543535.

George, G., Haas, M. R., & Pentland, A. (2014). *Big Data and Management.* Academy of Management Journal, 57(2), 321-326. doi:10.5465/amj.2014.4002.

Quinlan, J. R. (1979). *Discovering rules by induction from large collections of examples.* In D. Michie (Ed.), Expert systems in the micro electronic age. Edinburgh: Edinburgh University Press.

Quinlan, J. R. (1993). C4.5: *Programs for machine learning.* San Mateo, USA: Morgan Kaufmann Publishers.

Simon, H. A. (1967). *The Business School: A Problem In Organizational Design.* The Journal Of Management Studies, 4(1), 1-16.

Simsek, Z., Vaara, E., Paruchuri, S., Nadkarni, S., & Shaw, J. D. (2019). *New Ways of Seeing Big Data.* Academy of Management Journal, 62(4), 971-978. doi:10.5465/amj.2019.4004.

Vowels, S. A., & Goldberg, K. L. (Eds.). (2019). *Teaching Data Analytics: Pedagogy and Program Design.* New York,: CRC Press.

Wu, X., Kumar, V., Ross Quinlan, J., Ghosh, J., Yang, Q., Motoda, H., . Steinberg, D. (2007). *Top 10 algorithms in data mining. Knowledge and Information Systems*, 14(1), 1-37. doi:10.1007/s10115-007-0114-2.

Chapter

2

Whither Marketing? Three Emerging Topics

Zahra Sadeghinejad, Universal Business School Sydney

Arash Najmaei, Independent Consultant

ABSTRACT

Since the advent of the Digital Era, marketing departments have been placing increasing reliance on information and technologies from rapidly developing fields such as neuroscience and artificial intelligence and on social media to develop their marketing strategies. However, marketing education has not kept pace with these changes. This chapter addresses the widening gap between marketing practice and marketing education. The authors suggest that the gap can be narrowed by adding three new topics to traditional marketing curricula, namely, (1) neuromarketing, (2) humanistic marketing, and (3) artificial intelligence.

INTRODUCTION

Marketing science and education have always co-evolved with technological and social changes (Spais & Paul, 2021, p. 397). The current state of marketing theory is characterised by a heavy reliance on digital technologies, insights from other advanced fields like neuroscience and artificial intelligence, and social media (Huang & Rust, 2020). However, marketing education has fallen behind by not including some of the latest areas of knowledge in its curriculum. The purpose of this chapter is to address the shortfall.

To this end, the authors discuss three topics that they believe should be included in marketing curricula. They are (1) neuromarketing, (2) humanistic marketing, and (3) artificial intelligence. The authors explain each topic and discuss some of their key implications for the practice of marketing. They conclude by illustrating how mastering these three topics would add to the repertoire of skills required by marketing students who are preparing themselves for today's evolving job markets.

MARKETING 5.0 AND THE NEED FOR A NEW CURRICULUM

Marketing theory is going through its 5th generation. Marketing 5.0, known as marketing through technology for humanity (Kotler, Kartajaya, & Setiawan, 2021), extends previous generations where product-orientation (Marketing 1.0), consumer-orientation (Marketing 2.0), human-centrism (Marketing 3.0), and digital technology and social media (Marketing 4.0) defined marketing curricula. Marketing 5.0 has two distinct features: (1) unlike Marketing 4.0 where the emphasis was on basic digital technologies (Kotler, Kartajaya, & Setiawan, 2016), Marketing 5.0 focuses on more advanced technologies like big data analysis and artificial intelligence; and (2) it places special emphasis on a humanistic vision for marketing where values such as altruism, empathy, respect, trustworthiness, honesty, integrity, care, compassion, service, intelligence, beauty, and justice become the foundations of marketing theory, practice, and education (Kotler et al., 2021; Varey & Pirson, 2014). Marketing 5.0 necessities revolutionary changes to the way traditional marketing theory has been taught and practiced. Including the three emerging topics listed below can make marketing curricula more compatible with the vision of marketing 5.0.

NEUROMARKETING

Defining neuromarketing

The American Marketing Association (AMA) defines marketing as "an organizational function and a set of processes for creating, communicating, and delivering value to customers and for managing customer relationships in ways that benefit the organization and its stakeholders" (Grönroos, 2016, p. 397). Neuroscience helps marketers find better ways to create, communicate, and deliver value to stakeholders. It is a humanistic way of deciphering the complex world of consumer behaviour because it aims to understand emotions and feelings by studying their origins in the brain. The goal of neuromarketing is to adapt theories and methods from neuroscience and combine them with theories and methods from marketing and related disciplines, such as economics and psychology, to develop neuro-scientifically sound explanations of the impact of marketing on target customer behaviour (Lim, 2018).

Neuroscience uses a variety of techniques to decipher how our brain thinks, perceives, feels, and reacts to environmental stimuli.

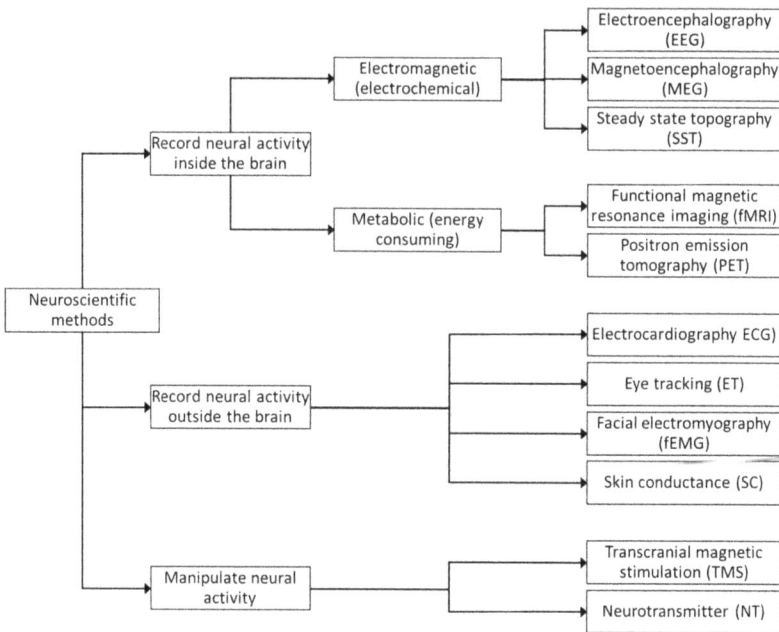

Figure 5 - a schematic illustration of the domain of techniques and tools used in neuroscience (Lim, 2018)

Applications of neuromarketing: some recent examples

Electroencephalography (ECC) is an electromagnetic technique that records neural activities such as responses to emotive photos or messages inside the brain (Lim, 2018). It captures how online consumers react to graphic emoticons known as emojis, an important function since 92% of online shoppers use emojis as intuitive and informal ways of expressing their emotions and attitudes toward brands, products, and other marketing offers (Hsu & Chen, 2021). Consumers' attention span is limited and is widely regarded as a key scarce resource for which marketers compete. Measuring how online users react to emojis reveals hidden information about their attitudes, mentalities, and perceptions, which can be then used in designing better marketing campaigns. Using ECC, Hsu and Chen (2021) found that placing emojis around an offering can have a significant influence on consumers' hotel selections, which was demonstrated by their altered neural activities.

Another application of neuromarketing is discussed in a study by Stasi et al. (2018), which addressed the intriguing issue of consumers' food choices. Decision-making about food benefits immensely from neuromarketing because it is often influenced by a complex set of emotions, feelings, attitudes, and values that are impossible to assess simply by asking consumers for their opinions (Stasi et al., 2018). Food marketers can use several technologies to explore how consumers make food choices. Some of the main neuromarketing tools used for this purpose are: (1) eye-tracking techniques to measure point-of-regard, eye movements, and visual attention; (2) Functional Magnetic Resonance Imaging (FMRI) and ECC to measure the metabolic activity in the brain in response to food-related stimuli; (3) Skin Conductance (SC) detection to measure the activity of the skin's sweat glands, which are controlled by the sympathetic branch of the Autonomic Nervous System (ANS); and (4) face-reading technologies to read and decipher facial expressions of consumers as indicators of their emotional state when they are exposed to a food/drink item. (See Stasi et al. (2018) for a comprehensive review of these neuromarketing techniques.)

HUMANISTIC MARKETING

Definition of humanistic marketing

Humanistic marketing stems from the paradigm of humanistic management (Kimakowitz, Pirson, Spitzeck, Dierksmeier, & Amann, 2011), according to which management theory and practice should advocate development of a global system for human dignity and well-being. Traditional marketing theory is based on the exchange paradigm from neo-classical theories of human beings. In this latter view, a human (e.g., a consumer) is a materialistic utility maximiser who values individual benefit over group and societal benefit - a 'homo economicus' who engages with others only in a transactional manner to promote his or her stable and predictable interests. He/she is amoral, values short-term gratification, and often acts opportunistically to further personal gain (Varey & Pirson, 2014). In this model, marketing is largely based on these limited and limiting assumptions and, in turn, is blamed for creating negative externalities such as unhealthy consumption patterns like smoking or overeating, and an increasingly consumerist and materialist society. This approach cherishes the "What I have" more than the "Who I am" and "What I do", resulting in widespread instances of depression, harm to society and the environment, and increasing inequalities (Varey & Pirson, 2014). Humanistic marketing advocates a paradigm shift. It "re-humanises by retiring the modern marketing ideology of domination, exploitation, unfettered growth, and raising to the fore: quality, truth, intelligence, conversation, and conditional growth" (Varey & Pirson, 2014, p. 276).

Applications of a humanistic approach in marketing

Humanistic marketing is a new paradigm. However, its applications are wide and numerous. For instance, humanistic advertising focuses on clear messages that promote healthy, environmentally friendly, and cruelty-free products. It highlights the adverse effects of over-consumption and of materialistic and impulsive purchases, shows health ratings, and explains ingredients of products and their potential harms. Similarly, humanistic pricing strategies avoid unethical pricing practices, include stakeholder modelling, and dynamically adapt to consumers' economic wellbeing. Humanistic product development differs from traditional product development strategies in at least three ways: 1) its focus on the physical and social wellbeing of consumers; 2) its objective of meeting previously unrecognized societal and environmental needs; and 3) its environmentally friendly treatment of design, production, and distribution. Humanistic marketing is also revolutionising market research by stressing more ethical and humanity-oriented research where the privacy, security, and dignity of consumers are important conditions of the research. All in all, marketing activities that rehumanise the previously dehumanised models of marketing are gaining momentum under this paradigm and are acting as liberating forces to change societies and markets toward a more sustainable future (Kotler et al., 2021).

ARTIFICIAL INTELLIGENCE IN MARKETING

What is artificial intelligence?

One of the characteristics of Marketing 5.0 is its use of human-mimicking technologies like artificial intelligence (Kotler et al., 2021). Artificial intelligence (AI) is an overarching term for advanced technologies that make computers act like people (Huang & Rust, 2020). It is often treated as a subfield of business intelligence and includes subdomains such as machine learning, cognitive computing, and deep learning (De Bruyn, Viswanathan, Beh, Brock, & von Wangenheim, 2020; Sterne, 2017).

According to Sterne (2017), an AI-enabled system has three main capabilities: 1) detecting most predictive attributes in a large dataset; 2) deliberating on the most important sources of data and weighing different attributes to make recommendations or draw reliable conclusions; and 3) developing a self-corrective and self-learning system where each iteration increases the maturity of the system and reduces its errors. As such, AI has a broad range of applications in facial recognition, visual recognition, voice recognition, natural language processing, expert systems, affective computing, and robotics - each with enormous potential to revolutionise marketing.

To better understand how AI advances marketing, Huang and Rust (2020) proposed a three-stage framework (see figure below) for strategic-marketing planning, incorporating multiple AI benefits: (1) mechanical AI for automating repetitive marketing functions and activities; (2) thinking AI for processing data to arrive at marketing decisions; and (3) feeling AI for analysing interactions and human emotions, particularly between an organisation and its customers.

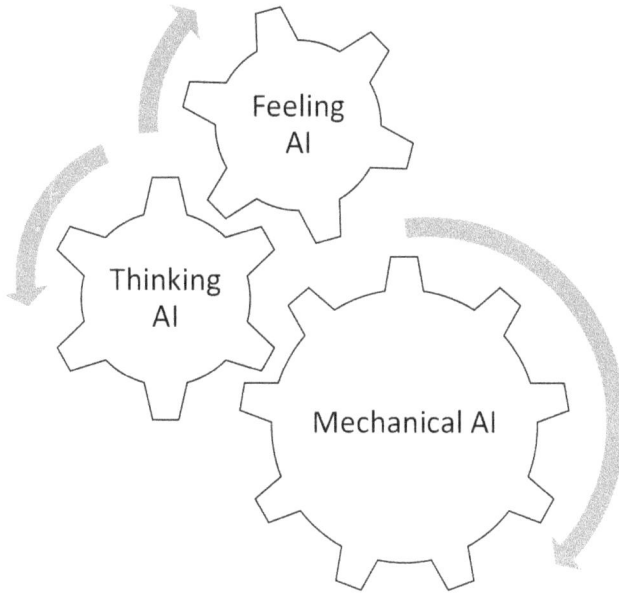

Figure 6 - Three types of artificial intelligence in marketing (Source: Huang & Rust, 2021)

Applications of AI in marketing

As noted by Huang and Rust (2020), applications of AI in marketing are on the rise due to increasing computing power, lower computing costs, the availability of big data from customers, suppliers, and other marketing stakeholders through social media, online sites, and tools like wearable devices, and the advance of machine-learning algorithms and models.

Marketers can apply three complementary types of AI. Mechanical AI is designed for automating repetitive and routine tasks like classification of customers, categorisation of product types in large distribution networks, and market segmentation. These applications accelerate execution of marketing strategies, speed up market research to develop new strategies, and enhance evaluation of planned marketing actions. Thinking AI is designed for processing data to arrive at new conclusions or decisions through methods such as text mining, speech recognition, voice recognition, and facial recognition. Marketers can use thinking AI to discover new needs, explore untapped market niches, formulate new offerings, and suggest new combinations of products and services. These benefits stem from the power of AI to identify previously unrecognised patterns in consumers' data from social media, hearing devices like smart speakers, and mobile phones. Finally, feeling AI is designed to analyse human feelings and emotions via techniques like sentiment analysis, natural language processing (NLP), and embedded virtual agents. Marketers can use feeling AI to explore how consumers think about a brand, how they feel about changes in profit designs, how they react emotionally to a marketing campaign, and how they perceive changes to product distribution placement and endorsement by celebrities. As such, feeling AI enables marketers to mimic consumers' emotions, to study them more accurately, and to utilise their learning in offering more appealing offerings.

CONCLUDING REMARKS

Marketing creates and delivers value. The sources of value and the methods of creating it evolve with socio-cultural and technological advances, and so should models and methods of teaching marketing education. In this chapter the authors proposed three themes that are aligned with the vision of the new generation of marketing theory (i.e., Marketing 5.0). They believe that inclusion of these themes in marketing curricula will equip marketing graduates with important tools needed to meet new sociocultural and technological challenges.

REFERENCES

De Bruyn, A., Viswanathan, V., Beh, Y. S., Brock, J. K.-U., & von Wangenheim, F. (2020). *Artificial Intelligence and Marketing: Pitfalls and Opportunities*. Journal of Interactive Marketing, 51, 91-105. doi:10.1016/j.intmar.2020.04.007.

Grönroos, C. (2016). *On defining marketing: finding a new roadmap for marketing*. Marketing Theory, 6(4), 395-417. doi:10.1177/1470593106069930.

Hsu, L., & Chen, Y.-J. (2021). *Neuromarketing, Subliminal Advertising, and Hotel Selection: An EEG Study*. Australasian Marketing Journal, 28(4), 200-208. doi:10.1016/j.ausmj.2020.04.009.

Huang, M.-H., & Rust, R. T. (2020). *A strategic framework for artificial intelligence in marketing*. Journal of the Academy of Marketing Science, 49(1), 30-50. doi:10.1007/s11747-020-00749-9.

Kimakowitz, E. v., Pirson, M., Spitzeck, H., Dierksmeier, C., & Amann, W. (Eds.). (2011). *Humanistic Management in Practice*. London, UK: Palgrave Macmillan.

Kotler, P., Kartajaya, H., & Setiawan, I. (2016). *Marketing 4.0: Moving from Traditional to Digital*. New York, USA: John Wiley & Sons.

Kotler, P., Kartajaya, H., & Setiawan, I. (2021). *Marketing 5.0 Technology for Humanity*. New York, USA: John Wiley & Sons.

Lim, W. M. (2018). *Demystifying neuromarketing*. Journal of Business Research, 91, 205-220. doi:10.1016/j.jbusres.2018.05.036.

Spais, G., & Paul, P. (2021). *A Crisis Management Model For Marketing Education: Reflections On Marketing Education System's Transformation In View Of The Covid-19 Crisis*. Marketing Education Review, 1-18.

Stasi, A., Songa, G., Mauri, M., Ciceri, A., Diotallevi, F., Nardone, G., & Russo, V. (2018). *Neuromarketing empirical approaches and food choice: A systematic review*. Food Res Int, 108, 650-664. doi:10.1016/j.foodres.2017.11.049.

Sterne, J. (2017). *Artificial Intelligence for Marketing: Practical Applications*. New York, NY: John Wiley & Sons.

Varey, R., & Pirson, M. (Eds.). (2014). *Humanistic Marketing*. London, UK: Palgrave Macmillan.

Chapter

3

New Considerations for Charting an Effective Business Plan

Art Phillips, Universal Business School Sydney

ABSTRACT

The author both heads a Centre for Entrepreneurship and teaches postgraduate students how to prepare entrepreneurship and business reports. In this chapter, he points out that the growth of new e-commerce sales and marketing platforms and tools, such as data-driven marketing, voice search engines, and Afterpay, along with the growing incidence of major shocks like COVID-19, have substantially changed the environment in which new businesses start and operate. He explains, with real-life examples, how he has changed the content and delivery of a postgraduate subject to accommodate these changes.

INTRODUCTION

Successful businesses require a business plan. The plan is a convenient vehicle for providing key information to investors and shareholders, and is an essential document for obtaining commercial loans. For both start-ups and established businesses, a business plan provides a continuing flow of information for the owner(s), and sets out the rationale for the business's goals and strategic plans. It describes the actions the owners will take to ensure the venture will sail safely through start-up phase and into the future. As stated by Alan Manly OAM, founder and CEO of Group Colleges Australia (GCA) and the Universal Business School Sydney (UBSS):

> *'A successful business plan encapsulates a great new idea and a path to bring that idea to fruition'* (Manly, 2021).

From 2019, the author has been teaching the subject **Entrepreneurship Research Report** (MCR012) at the Universal Business School Sydney (UBSS). During the preceding two years, he was the subject's grading adjudicator. Over his 5-year association with the subject, he has observed significant changes in the business environment. Of particular significance are the new AI marketing platforms such as Chatbots, CamFind, Voice Search, and Snapchat; the new sales platforms like AfterPay and ZipPay; and the new and/or improved media platforms such as TikTok, Instagram, Facebook, and YouTube. Further, due to faster Internet speeds in Australia since the roll-out of the National Broadband Network (NBN), consumers have become increasingly comfortable with buying goods and services online. E-commerce, in all its forms, is growing and changing rapidly. IbisWorld, Industry Research Reports (Australia) states:

> *"Revenue for the Online Shopping industry is anticipated to rise by 35.3% in the current year due to more bricks-and-mortar firms establishing online operations"* (June 2021).

Entrepreneurship Research Report has three strands that align neatly with the content requirements of a standard business plan, namely, the *Executive Summary* (about the business – the why, how, aim and structure), *Marketing* (analysis of market competitors and design of marketing campaigns), and *Finance* (assumptions, forecasts, and projections of sales and costs associated with funding and running the business). In the following sections, the author identifies how his teaching content has been influenced by the growth of new sales, delivery, and marketing platforms, as well as by the increasing demand for online shopping using new technologies.

The chapter also considers contingency measures that should be written into business plans to provide security against devasting events such as the COVID-19 pandemic and the ensuing lockdowns. These events raise new concerns for businesses, and contingency structures need to be developed that reach far beyond traditional strategic thinking. Thus, the new business plan must extend beyond simply designing measures to deal with 'competition', or the effects of disruptive business events, or with changes in customer-centric product lines. Well-designed survival strategies must be written into the business plans if companies are to survive and thrive in the new and more precarious 2020s financial environment.

The author's entrepreneurship subject is designed to prepare postgraduate students for the real business world by providing them with four key learning outcomes. Upon completion of the subject, students should be able to:

- *Identify* the major requirements in the process of preparing effective and practical business plans
- *Evaluate* the process of setting goals, explaining objectives, and mapping out how to achieve these goals with strategic actions
- *Develop* the techniques needed to explain why the business vision is a valuable opportunity, how to report on resources required, who will implement the vision, and how the goals will be reached; and
- *Implement* techniques to show how risks to the business vision will be mitigated and how unexpected opportunities may be exploited.

A vital support for a business is a clear business vision that is both inspiring and realistic. The mission, vision, and executive summary must *tell a compelling story* that demonstrates how the business will succeed. The subject allows students to understand and implement the strategies needed to move from a business vision (an idea that is unique and has a competitive edge) to a practical business plan (a solid blueprint or roadmap with forecasting arrows) for a successful company.

The three strands of **Entrepreneurship Research Report** require innovative thinking by students as they design a business plan that is appropriate for the 2020s.

STRAND 1 – EXECUTIVE SUMMARY (WEEKS 1 ~ 4)

Description

The first section of the course focuses on teaching students how to think about unique business opportunities and how to clearly identify and describe how and why the business will succeed in today's complex and competitive environment. It is essential that students have a passion for implementing their business idea. Of course, passion is not sufficient - focus, determination, and perseverance are also required. Throughout his entire life and business career, the author has supported his passion for business ventures with the 3-letter mantra: 'FDP' = Focus, Determination, and Perseverance.

There are other important requirements for success in the modern business environment. The prospective entrepreneur must consider the huge number of products in the world (there are several million in the NATO database), and the extraordinary saturation of most of the products being manufactured and sold by so many different companies (estimated to exceed 100 million). Therefore, the business each student chooses must pass the following tests:

- It must create and sell a product that is unique and meets a need that is not currently being addressed, or a product that will compete with existing products but can be made and sold better
- It must be able to attract the finance required to get the venture off the ground and sustain the business until it makes a profit
- It must be environmentally friendly; and

- The student, the entrepreneur, must be passionate about the product and the purpose of the business.

Changes

In today's world it is important to ensure that a business has more than a 'shopfront' location. E-commerce, with its new forms of online sales and marketing platforms, is now critical for survival. In our COVID-19 world, keeping up-to-date with the new trends in e-commerce can be a business lifesaver. Online sales have long been an important part of business activities, but now and more than ever, it is necessary to embrace online sales using new technologies in order to secure business sustainability.

Examples

With the business world being saturated with goods and services, the prospective entrepreneur needs a product that is unique and meets a pressing consumer need. These two considerations account for about 80% of business success; the remaining 20% can be attributed to luck.

The author's subject requires that students work with a business concept. Some come to the first class with a clearly developed concept. Those who don't are required to identify a concept by using brain-storming methodology to fill the gaps in the following three statements:

- The three things I find most annoying are (1) _____ (2) _____ (3) _____.
- Every single time I use (product) _____, I find (what) _____so frustrating.
- There's no app for _____. What could I provide to fill the gap _____?

For example, one thing that really annoys the author is going to a restaurant or a coffee shop and finding that the legs on the table he sits at are not perfectly aligned with the floor, causing the table to rock when he leans on it. He had developed a solution to this problem over 30 years ago - a wedge that could be inserted between a table leg and the floor. The wedge could be stored and carried on a key ring and so would always be available. However, a patent for his discovery had already been registered by another inventor; hence, the author's application for a patent was rejected. Then, three months later, he saw the patented product in a local hardware shop. However, the availability of the product has not been sufficient to solve the problem. Waiters still respond to customer complaints by inserting a folded paper napkin or a cardboard coaster between the table leg and the floor. Perhaps it is time for some enterprising student to complete the solution to the problem!

Most business ideas arise from experiencing dissatisfaction with existing products and situations, asking questions, conducting extensive research, and coming up with solutions. In an article, *Six ways to come up with your ultimate business idea*, The Guardian advised:

> *'If you look around your house or workplace, you'll see a huge number of problems or mundane tasks that could potentially be made easier by a new product or service. If you identify an issue that someone else hasn't already solved, chances are there will be a market for it' (Lottie O'Conor, The Guardian, 2015).*

Once their business ideas are set, students are required to create a clever business name that has meaning – subconsciously or consciously. It is also necessary that a trademark and various registrations can be obtained for the name. The author uses his own business - a music production company – as an example. This company was created with the name 101 Music Pty Ltd®. As numbers usually precede letters in alpha-listings, the name puts his business at the top of the list with the author's 24 distributor/sub-publisher/agent websites. The name also meshes with the '101 ways to _____' style of presentation, such as '101 ways to teach your dog new tricks' and '101 ways to cook the greatest Italian food'. It meets the "one better" condition, where 101 subconsciously gives the user a feeling of gaining more 'value' than

**Figure 7 - logo of 101 Music
(https://101.audio)**

100. The name also contains the binary numbers 1 and 0, giving a high-tech feel to the label.

The author then has his students construct a short sales 'slogan' that fits with the business name, using that for his own company - *emotional solutions through music* – as an example.

STRAND 2 – MARKETING (WEEKS 5 ~ 8)

Description

Developing and implementing promotional marketing strategies is at the heart of this section. Effective marketing involves the analysis of the business's major competitors and target customers, and the design and creation of advertising campaigns to capture customers' attention. It therefore requires a deep understanding of customer needs and awareness.

Changes

The author requires students to develop a marketing strategy that exploits the potential of new and emerging marketing platforms. Recently, a multitude of new platforms has been developed, most of which are AI-based. As the Single Grain digital marketing website states:

> *"Artificial intelligence is the biggest commercial opportunity for companies, industries, and nations over the next few decades. A.I. latecomers will find themselves at a serious competitive disadvantage within the next several years" (David, 2021).*

Single Grain (Digital marketing trends in 2021), also noted that:

> *"At one time, artificial intelligence, data-driven marketing and voice search engine optimization (VSEO) were ambitious concepts bordering on the ridiculous. Today, these innovative digital marketing trends are among the top priorities for most business owners in 2021.*
>
> *And why wouldn't they be? After all, if your business has any intention of remaining competitive in today's online landscape, you must adapt to the rapidly evolving changes in digital marketing"* (David, 2021).

Some amazing new methods of high-tech marketing platforms will be coming our way in the 2020s, including metaverse, which uses alternative digital realities depending on where people work, play, and socialise. In July 2020, Forbes' web-edition stated:

> *'Imagine walking down the street. Suddenly, you think of a product you need. Immediately next to you, a vending machine appears, filled with the product and variations you were thinking of. You stop, pick an item from the vending machine, it's shipped to your house, and then continue on your way'* (Hackl, 2021).

In late June 2021, Mark Zuckerberg, CEO of Facebook, told his employees about an ambitious new initiative, saying:

> *"The future of the company would go far beyond its current project of building a set of connected social apps and some hardware to support them. Instead, he said, Facebook would strive to build a maximalist, interconnected set of experiences straight out of sci-fi world, known as the* **metaverse.**
>
> *The company's divisions focused on products for communities, creators, commerce, and virtual reality - (and that we) would increasingly work to realize these visions. What I think is most interesting is how these themes will come together into a bigger idea. Our overarching goal across all of these initiatives is to help bring the metaverse to life"* (Zuckerberg, 2021).

The author also discusses with his students the need for distinctive 'wordsmithing' in marketing - using emotional keywords to grab the audience's attention. For illustration, he points out that in his own business he uses 'keywords' as emotional descriptives, which are included in his extensive metadata excel spreadsheets on release of each album product. He uses key adjectives, adverbs, and the like to stir the five senses that help navigate the user to his product.

STRAND 3 – FINANCES (WEEKS 9 ~ 12)

Description

The final segment of the course deals with forecasting, assumptions, and projections of business finance. Students are required to analyse competitors' behaviour and to employ a competitive strategy with pricing. They identify a pricing strategy, forecast how much they can sell in a day, week, month, and year, and compare sales with manufacturing costs (direct costs) to achieve a workable Gross Profit Margin. They then outline projected fixed costs (indirect costs - the day-to-day costs of running the business) to derive a forecasted Operating Profit Margin. Finally, they include tax and interest expenses in order to generate a Net Profit Margin. This exercise ensures that the students understand 'break-even analysis' and know how to chart, analyse, and 'massage' pricing and costings so they can successfully launch their businesses.

Changes

The new marketing and sale technologies will have a big impact on business formation, growth, and sustainability in the coming decade. The changes being implemented in the author's Entrepreneurship course include incorporation of the newest platforms for purchasing such as 'Afterpay'. Whether sales are made instore or online, this facility provides consumers who are short of funds with the opportunity to take their purchases home with them or have the purchases shipped immediately. With Afterpay, customers can pay in four instalments over six weeks, with the first payment collected at the time of purchase – all interest free. The retailers are paid within just a few days of the purchases, and Afterpay take on the risk of fraud. Retailers also receive settlement reports every day to reconcile orders and sales. This new payment method will become part of the new business environment, since:

> *"Afterpay partners see a 20% increase in cart conversion on average, and more repeat customers. Afterpay lets customers get what they want, when they want it, increasing (the) average order value by up to 40%" (Afterpay, 2021).*

John Strain, Chief Digital and Technology Officer, Gap Inc supports this view. He states that:

> *"By adding Afterpay to our other payment options, we're able to provide a more customized shopping experience, give our customers additional convenience and control and reach a younger demographic who may not have been able to shop with us before" (Strain, 2021).*

It is increasingly important for students to experience the real world in order to better understand the internal mechanics of a successful business. Therefore, in early 2021, the author introduced interview style guest presentations to the classroom (Phillips, 2021). He also added a short discussion about the various accounting systems, such as Xero and MYOB, and the use of 'bank feeds' to streamline account processing, BAS compliance and submissions, as well as PAYG tax and single touch payroll. The bank feed system is a great time saver, allowing businesses to spend more time on their product lines and marketing.

CONCLUSION

In this day and age, digital technologies are changing as fast as the seconds pass. It is therefore essential for established and prospective entrepreneurs to read, research, and explore the ever-evolving business world and to incorporate new and emerging threats and opportunities into their business plan. The plan is an evolving document that must change in line with the changing business environment.

The author concludes his final lecture with the challenging message:

> *Hurdles are our friends.*
>
> *Disappointments are never our enemy*

REFERENCES

Afterpay, (2021). *https://www.afterpay.com/en-US/for-retailers*

Dave, N. (2021). *42 Digital Marketing Trends You Can't Ignore in 2021.* *https://www.singlegrain.com/digital-marketing/digital-marketing-trends-2021/*

Drucker, P. (2015). *Innovation and Entrepreneurship*, Routledge. *https://www.routledge.com/Innovation-and-Entrepreneurship/Drucker/p/book/*

Hackl, C. (2021). CMO Network. *https://www.forbes.com/sites/cathyhackl/2020/07/05/the-metaverse-is-coming--its-a-very-big-deal/?sh=6e516d38440f*

IBIS World (2021). *Online Shopping in Australia – Market Research Report. https://www.ibisworld.com/au/industry/online-shopping/1837*

Llopis, G. (2013). *Forbes, Leadership Strategy.* *https://www.forbes.com/sites/glennllopis/2013/04/01/12-things-successfully-convert-a-great-idea-into-a-reality/?sh=77fb9f024e86*

Manly, A. (2021). *A Simple Plan, Inside Small Business.* *https://insidesmallbusiness.com.au/management/a-simple-plan*

OBERLO statistics (2021). Global e-commerce sales, cited: *https://au.oberlo.com/statistics/global-ecommerce-sales*

O'Connor, L. (2021). *https://www.theguardian.com/small-business-network/2015/jul/31/six-ways-become-entreprenuer-business-idea*

Phillips, A. (2021). *Interview Style Guest Presentations that Enhance Learning. https://www.ubss.edu.au/media/2785/interview-style-guest-presentations-that-enhance-learning.pdf*

Strain, J. (2021). *https://www.afterpay.com/en-US/for-retailers*

TechCrunch (2020). *https://techcrunch.com/2020/08/24/covid-19-pandemic-accelerated-shift-to-e-commerce-by-5-years-new-report-says*

Zuckerberg, M. (2021). *https://www.theverge.com/22588022/mark-zuckerberg-facebook-ceo-metaverse-interview*

Chapter

4

The Growing Concerns About Technological Unemployment

Angus Hooke, Universal Business School Sydney

Harpreet Kaur, Australian Institute of Higher Education

ABSTRACT

Academics are continually updating their courses to reflect changes in the content (structure and behaviour) of their discipline, the understanding by the academic community of this content, and the content needs of the students who are enrolled in the course. In this chapter, two authors who teach an undergraduate course in Economics at a higher education institution in Sydney discuss the increasing importance of technological unemployment, and how they have changed the content of their course to accommodate this development.

INTRODUCTION

The content of an academic course can change because the subject matter of the discipline has changed, the academic community's understanding of that subject matter has changed, or the requirements of those taking the course have changed. Examples include the effects of the COVID-19 pandemic on the discipline of medicine, our better understanding of the relationship between the burning of fossil fuels and average global temperature on the discipline of climate science, and the switching of automobile demand from petrol-driven to electricity-driven cars on the discipline of automotive engineering. In Economics, they include the growing impact of new technologies on unemployment, our greater appreciation of the role of budget deficits on economic management (Modern Monetary Theory), and the ageing of populations on welfare analysis. In this chapter, the authors discuss some of the changes they have made to an undergraduate course in Economics in response to the growing impact of, and concern about, technological unemployment.

A BRIEF HISTORY OF TECHNOLOGICAL UNEMPLOYMENT

The concept of technological unemployment is not new. More than two millennia ago, Aristotle (384-322 BCE) observed that:

> *"If every instrument could accomplish its own work, obeying or anticipating the will of others, … if, in like manner, the shuttle would weave and the plectrum touch the lyre without a hand to guide them, chief workmen would not want servants, nor masters' slaves."* *(Medved, 2015)*

Nor is fear of technological unemployment a new phenomenon. In 1589 an Englishman named William Lee made the first stocking-frame-knitting machine. (He made it, not because he was a dyed-in-the wool entrepreneur, but because a young girl he was courting was showing more interest in knitting than in him.) Twice William asked Queen Elizabeth I to grant him a patent for his invention. Twice the Queen denied his request, the second time stating:

> *"Thou aimest high, Master Lee. Consider thou what the invention could do to my poor subjects. It would assuredly bring to them ruin by depriving them of employment, thus making them beggars." (Laskow, 2017)*

Concern about the impact of technology on employment reached a peak in the northern counties of England in the early 19th century. In 1811, a group of six workers broke into a hosiery factory in

Nottingham. They waited until midnight and then, using large wooden hammers and timing their blows so the sound was drowned out by the striking of the town clock, smashed as many machines as they could in the short time available to them. Their action sparked a wave of similar attacks throughout the English Midlands. When the police arrived at the factories and asked who had destroyed the machines, the workers would reply "It must have been Ned Ludd!", referring to the intellectually challenged son of a textile worker in Nottingham who, in 1799, had smashed two textile frames. Their answer to the police brought possibly unwanted fame to Ned, with the anti-technology movement now often referred to, disparagingly, as the *Luddite Movement* and its adherents described as *Luddites.*

The term, technological unemployment, is generally attributed to the famous English economist John Maynard Keynes who, during the Great Depression, when more than 30% of the European and North American workforces were unemployed, wrote:

> *"We are being afflicted by a new disease ... technological unemployment. This means unemployment due to our discovery of means of economising the use of labour outrunning the pace at which we can find new uses for labour." (Keynes, 1930)*

However, during the Industrial Era (1800-2000), the fears of the Luddites – and of Keynes -seemed to be unfounded. Over this 200-year period, cyclically adjusted unemployment in Europe and North America was reasonably stable at about 5% of the work force. The share of wages in GDP was also roughly unchanged at around 60% (the share in NDP – Net Domestic Product – which subtracts depreciation from GDP, was higher, at about 75%). The prevailing view among labour market economists was that technological change affected the composition of the demand for labour, but not its level (Autor, 2015). In an analysis of data from 21 developed countries for 1985–2009, Feldmann (2013) concluded that technological innovations did give rise to a short-term rise in unemployment, but overall unemployment returned to its original level after about three years. Hence, Economics courses in the late 20th and early 21st centuries tended either to ignore technological unemployment or to use it as an example of the failure of non-economists to understand the nature and strength of the adjustment mechanisms that operate in flexible labour markets. Those who expressed deep concern about technological unemployment were accused of being guilty of the Luddite Fallacy.

However, during the middle part of the Industrial Era there was a harbinger of what many think now might be the fate of the human workforce in the current era - the Digital Era. At the turn of the 20th century, England had two great work forces - horses and humans - each with about 3 million members. The invention and popularity of automobiles and electricity then caused the demand for work horses to fall dramatically. Initially, this impacted on the real wage of the horses – the quantity and quality of their feed. (Horses were notably thinner in 1920 than in 1900). Then, the rise of the new technologies affected the number of horses, which fell to a few hundred thousand by 2030. Now England has only about 50,000 horses, and they are used mainly for racing or kept as pets.

TECHNOLOGICAL UNEMPLOYMENT AND THE DIGITAL ERA

Signs that technology might be having a larger effect on employment – specifically, automation on manual jobs and artificial intelligence (AI) on cognitive jobs - began to emerge toward the end of the Industrial Era. In the United States, the share of workers who had not received a wage increase in the preceding decade rose from about 10% in 1980 to 30% in 2000. By 2016, when Donald Trump was courting unskilled and semi-skilled workers in the "rust-belt" states, the ratio was close to 50%.

Many recent studies support the view that job destruction due to technological change will increase and that the number of jobs destroyed will be high. The most prominent and oft-cited of these is the seminal study by Carl Benedikt Frey and Michael Osborne (2013), which estimated that 47% of the US workforce was under high risk (70% probability or more) of losing their jobs to computerization (automation by computer-controlled equipment) in the succeeding decades. Following widespread dissemination of this study, other researchers applied a similar methodology in other countries, with equally concerning results: UK (35%), Canada

(42%), Germany (42%), Switzerland (48%), Uzbekistan (55%), Brazil (60%), and Ethiopia (85%) (Lima et al, 2021).

On the other hand, technological change creates new jobs, and one major study suggests that, in the short run at least, it could produce a net increase in jobs. The Future of Jobs Report (WEF, 2018). which was commissioned by the World Economic Forum, surveyed a group of companies employing about 15 million workers and found that while these companies expected technological change to destroy about one million of their jobs in the five-year period ending 2022, they also predicted that it would create about 1.75 million additional jobs during the same period.

The longer-run outlook is more pessimistic. Some economists and most futurists, applying Moore's Law or plausible variants of it to technological change, believe it is inevitable that, at some future date, machines and algorithms will be able to perform all jobs – physical, mental, and emotional – much more quickly and at lower cost than can natural (i.e., unenhanced) biological humans. Calum Chase points that, if machines continue to double in capability every 18 month (Moore's law), they will be 100 times more powerful in 10 years, 8 thousand times more powerful in 20 years, and more than a million times more powerful in 30 years. Eventually, he argues, technology will lead to natural, biological humans becoming unemployable.

CHANGES IN COURSE CONTENT

The discipline of economics can be divided into six areas: the two microeconomic areas of resource allocation and income distribution; and the four macroeconomic areas of unemployment, inflation, the balance of payments, and economic growth. The unemployment component of the course taught by the two authors focuses on the types, causes, and effects of unemployment, and on policies that can be implemented to address unemployment. Earlier versions of the course either ignored technological unemployment or used it as one example of structural employment. The current version of the course treats it as a self-contained and major type of unemployment. Below, the authors provide some examples of policies they discuss with students that address the issue of rising technological unemployment. The policies are divided into ameliorating and coping policies.

Ameliorating policies are designed to reduce technological unemployment. On the labour supply side, policy makers might try to speed up the secular decline in the number of hours people work. While many of us claim to be working harder and longer than ever, we may be fooling ourselves. In 1800, in the countries that now form the Organisation for Economic Cooperation and Development (OECD), a typical adult worked about 4,000 hours a year. By 2000, the number had fallen to 1,832 hours, a reduction of about 11 hours a year over the 200-year period. During the first two decades of this century, the average working year in the OECD area declined by a further seven hours a year, to 1,687 hours in 2020 (see table below). Accelerating the substitution of leisure for work would reduce the magnitude of the challenge faced by policies aimed at lowering technological unemployment by increasing the demand for labour.

Table 1 - Hours worked per worker per year in the OECD area, 2000-20
(Source: OECD)

	2000	2005	2010	2015	2020	Annual change
OECD	1,832	1,792	1,772	1,764	1,687	-7
USA	1,832	1,792	1,772	1,783	1,767	-3
Australia	1,873	1,820	1,778	1,751	1,683	-9
Germany	1,488	1,447	1,426	1,401	1,332	-8
Denmark	1,471	1,452	1,422	1,407	1,346	-6
Japan	1,823	1,778	1,733	1,719	1,598	-11
Korea	2,479	2,321	2,163	2,083	1,908	-29

On the demand side, the most promising policy might be to encourage innovation and entrepreneurship. In Australia, the secular supply of labour is currently increasing by about 150,000 workers a year. At the same time, existing firms are shedding a net 50,000 workers a year. But unemployment is not rising by 200,000 every year. Just as they have done since the start of the Industrial Era, new firms are filling the gap. Switching government support from subsidising existing firms to support old jobs (e.g., Holden) to providing a more favourable environment for innovation and entrepreneurship, especially in digitally based products, could be expected to stimulate the overall demand for labour.

But, as Calum Chase notes, eventually the power of Moore's Law or some variant of it may dominate our best efforts to contain technological unemployment. A very large proportion of the population will probably become unemployable. As with COVID-19, eventually we will have to live with the problem. We will need coping policies. The authors address this worst-case scenario (or best-case scenario, depending on one's standpoint on the intrinsic value of work) and discuss with students how an income can be provided to the population when there is limited or no market-based work for biological humans. This leads to a discussion of the basic income scheme, which uses the output generated by the machines to provide a minimum weekly or monthly income based on only one criterion – residency or citizenship.

The authors complete this segment of the course by considering one more coping measure, often referred to as the Merging of Man and Machine (MMM), or the "Join them!" measure. Students are invited to discuss scenarios in which biological and synthetic enhancements to originally natural humans might narrow and then eliminate the work-place advantages of the machines, describe timelines for different outcomes, assign probabilities to the outcomes and timelines, and consider the short- and longer-term implications for their own careers.

CONCLUSION

It has always been desirable to keep the content of business courses up to date. However, with the increasing pace of change, what was once a leisurely and occasional activity has now become an urgent and continuing requirement. This chapter has shown how an issue of growing concern in the field of Economics – technological unemployment - has been incorporated into an undergraduate course in a manner that students have found to be both engaging and useful. It can serve as an example of how future changes in the content of the discipline can be addressed.

REFERENCES

Autor, D.H. (2015). *Why Are There Still So Many Jobs? The History and Future of Workplace Automation.* Journal of Economic Perspectives. Vol. 29, No. 3, Summer. Pp. 3-30.

Chase, C. (2018). *The Economic Singularity.* *https://www.youtube.com/watch?v=FZh_SzVDQVI*

Ford, M. (2015*). Rise of the robots: Technology and the threat of a jobless future.* New York: Basic Books.

Keynes, John Maynard. (1930). *Economic Possibilities for our Grandchildren.* *https://medium.com/8vc-news/the-future-of-labor-pt-i-keynes-f3ae0f2808b6*

Kurt, R. (2019*). Industry 4.0 in Terms of Industrial Relations and Its Impacts on Labour Life.* Procedia Computer Science. Volume 158, pp 590-601. *https://doi.org/10.1016/j.procs.2019.09.093*

Laskow, S. (2017). *A machine that made stockings helped kick off the industrial revolution.* *https://www.atlasobscura.com/articles/machine-silk-stockings-industrial-revolution-queen-elizabeth*

Lima, Y.; Barbosa, C.E.; dos Santos, H.S.; de Souza, J.M. (2021). *Understanding Technological Unemployment: A Review of Causes, Consequences, and Solutions.* Societies. 11, 50. *https://doi.org/10.3390/soc11020050*

Chapter

5

The impact of the Pandemic on Marketing Practices

Felix Stravens, Universal Business School Sydney

ABSTRACT

COVID 19 has changed consumer behaviour and buying patterns. Marketers therefore need to find new ways to reach out to consumers and get them to buy products. The 4Ps – Product, Price, Place, and Promotion - developed by Philip Kotler, is still relevant in marketing but some of the Ps now have a different meaning. During the pandemic, the 4Ps have morphed into Product, Price, People and Process. With marketers now grappling with the People and Process requirements, academics must ensure that students are properly trained to meet this new focus of marketing practice, especially the Process component.

INTRODUCTION

From its outset, the COVID-19 pandemic has been changing the way marketers build brands and develop customer relationships. There was a sudden rise in e-commerce. In 2020, the increase was 20% in Europe (double the rate in 2019) and in the United States it was 32%. E-commerce is continuing to grow rapidly in 2021.

CUSTOMERS

Before the pandemic, marketing used to start with knowing the customer. Using Demographics, marketers gauged the size of the potential market for their product and selected mass media to provide a broad coverage of the target market. However, whilst Demographics showed the size of the market, it did not indicate how to reach buyers effectively.

Marketers then moved into Psychographics to understand their target market's activities, interests, and opinions (AIO). The information was then used to tailor messages that reflected their customers' lifestyles and appealed to them.

Since the onset of the pandemic, it has been necessary for marketers to refocus the aims of their campaigns. Instead of placing emphasis on the potential target market, they have had to focus on the particular segment of the market they wished to appeal to. This meant truly understanding the situation on the ground when appealing to customers. It meant harnessing not only psychographics but also attitudinal characteristics of the target segment.

During the pandemic consumers have been worried about the health of their families, whether they can afford their basic needs, and the loss of freedom. Research done by EY indicates that Australian consumers have the following focus:

- *Affordability*: Six in ten Australians plan to be more aware and cautious of their spending in the longer term and say price will be the most important purchase criterion for them three years from now. Their focus is on living within their means and budgets. They are looking at products they can afford without stretching their budgets. This has meant switching brands and even compromising on quality, if necessary. They have been focusing less on brands and more on the functionality of the product.
- *Health*: Over one in two (55%) want to make healthier choices in their product purchases in the longer term and say health or 'what's good for me' will be the most important criterion. Protecting their health and that of their family. They have been selecting products they trust to be

safe and looking for ways to minimise risks when they shop.

- *Sustainability*: 45% will prioritise the environment and climate change in how they live and the products they buy. The environmental impact of their purchasing is causing them to seek environmentally safe products.
- *Social Impact*: One in two (51%) will be more likely to buy from companies that ensure what they do has a positive impact on society. Some 36% will buy from responsible marketers especially those that appear to be honest and transparent, even if their products are more expensive.
- *Experiences*: 33% will be less inclined to get involved in experiences outside the home on account of health and safety concerns. Consumers want to make the most of life and are open to buying new products and trying new experiences. Some 59% stated they have changed the way they are entertained.

COMPETITORS

As customers have become more demanding, marketers are not just dealing with their competitors, they are also trying to ensure that the consumer gets the best experience from using their product. Marketing has become more experiential as marketers need to compete with the best experience the customer has had. It becomes more about personalisation and experience and the need to anticipate customer needs across the entire purchase and usage journey. There is, therefore, a need to ensure better collection of customer personal data and use this information to support the appeal throughout the journey.

Customers expect marketers to provide exactly what they want. They expect that any experience will be frictionless, anticipated, and relevant. Marketers therefore need to examine the use of artificial intelligence (AI) to obtain the necessary data to create relevant experiences for the customer. Marketers now must court their customers, and this means moving away from brand marketing and getting into performance marketing.

Marketers have always tried to ensure that customers are at the heart of the marketing journey. Now it has become even more essential as customers demand a good experience. Using overseas call centres or chatbots does not give customers the feeling that they are being courted. It is therefore important that marketers ensure that technology and talent are correctly aligned around the customers' needs.

Relationships are everything. Trust and integrity in marketers drive the demand for products. Marketers who listen to the voice of the customer and ensure that their product meets the consumer's needs can build both.

CHANGES IN MARKETING PRACTICE

Based on the consumer concerns outlined earlier, whilst Product is still important, consumers are tending to focus on products they can afford and not pay too much attention to the brand. They are also focusing on products that do not harm the environment. More importantly, their focus has switched to experiential. They are considering how they feel when they consume and their last experience with the product is determining their next purchase. Therefore, companies are not only competing with other competitors, they are also competing with themselves to maintain the on-going good feeling customers get from consuming their product.

In terms of *Price*, consumers are buying what they can afford. During these difficult times, they are focusing on value for money and affordability. Nevertheless, their main focus remains on product functionality.

Place used to be very important as marketers relied on distributors and retailers to ensure that their product was in the right place. With COVID-19 and the accompanying lockdowns, distribution has moved into the digital world. Products are being ordered online, without being physically examined by buyers, and are being moved by contactless delivery methods. Consumers no longer visit a retail outlet to examine a product, try it, and pick up what they want. They must make a quantum leap into the new digital world and make their e-commerce transaction. Whilst Generation Z may be comfortable with this method of purchase, most consumers including the Baby Boomers and higher-income consumers are in a completely new world of purchasing.

For *Promotions*, marketers used to simply go with mass media. If the budget was large enough, this approach would give them a good coverage of the target market with sufficient repetition. This has given gave way to selective media that more effectively reaches consumers. Once again, COVID-19 has changed everything as marketers move online to reach consumers who are at home.

SO, HOW SHOULD WE GO FORWARD TO ENSURE SUCCESSFUL MARKETING?

Product is important. Customers expect marketers to have exactly what they want. No compromise. This means that marketers must have data and technology at the heart of their organisation. The data will ensure that marketers are able to anticipate consumer wants and provide them with a more relevant experience. Customers are living in the moment to make the most of life and this makes them open to new products and new experiences.

Price will continue to play a major role in product selection. Consumers will continue to focus on value for money and marketers will have to demonstrate how the value is delivered. The brand must stand behind great value. Consumers will be looking not only at price but also at trust for the brand. Linked with that, consumers will also prefer to purchase from companies that practice ethical sourcing and demonstrate corporate social responsibility.

Whilst previously *Place* was important, this has now given way to a new P, *Process*. This means ensuring the e-commerce platform provides a good experience. It must be easy to use and fast. It also means generating online community involvement, ensuring potential customers have access to previous customer feedback. In the past, not many companies participated in e-commerce, as they did not see the need for it. Banking probably had the highest penetration followed by entertainment and media. Consumers are now used to buying online and they expect to do more of it in the future. This means that companies must reconsider their processes and perhaps even examine the possibility of cross-promoting products. This could mean that food companies cross-promote pharmaceutical products and encourage consumers to buy other products through their website. Woolworths recently announced that it would be tying up with specialist companies to offer their customers the opportunity to buy fashion products through the Woolworths site.

The final P – *Promotions*, has given way to *People*. Consumers need to be courted and won. Customer Relation Management (CRM) now has increased importance. While advertising can create a promise for the product, the latter will have to deliver on the promise. However, the customer experience is the key to whether consumers re-purchase the product. As most transactions are now executed in an online environment, relationships must be properly maintained. Trust and integrity are fundamental to success. These allow marketers to listen to the consumer, both the good and the bad feedback, and then deliver solutions that meet the consumers' needs.

CONCLUSION

Marketing continues to be both an art and a science. In these uncertain times, there is a need to have a balance between humans and automation. Relevant, up-to-date, and reliable data are important for understanding consumers and anticipating their needs. At the same time, marketers need to maintain a brand that reflects honesty and integrity and offers great value. Marketers will need to focus on how people live and not on what they buy.

With the customer at the centre of all activity, we need to ensure proper Consumer Social Responsibility. Using IT to collect information and building a reliable and easy-access platform can ensure that the lifetime value (LTV) of customers will increase and they will remain loyal.

Digital adoption, or e-commerce, has grown rapidly and has changed the behaviour and expectations of consumers. It can be expected that this trend will continue as more consumers accept e-commerce as the new normal.

So how does this impact on the teaching of marketing?

Academics will need to learn and impart new knowledge and skills to their students. They will need to teach:

Agility. Marketers will need to find out if the message being sent to customers is appropriate. They will need to ensure that the supply chain is functioning correctly. They will have to be nimble and take prompt corrective action when problems occur. This agility includes active listening and sensing by the whole company to capture consumer sentiment.

Brand should stand behind great values. The EY Future Consumer Index found that up to 61% of consumers, depending on the category, were not only willing to switch brands, but also were prepared to consider a white label product. This means that brands should focus on the values they express.

Key themes from the EY Research show that "while quality, convenience, and price still very much matter to consumers choice, factors like sustainability, trust, ethical sourcing, and social responsibility are increasingly important to how consumers select their products and services."

To be successful, companies need to ensure that marketing is everyone's responsibility. They must realise that the home is now a multifunctional hub. It is now a place where consumers live, work, learn, shop, and play. Marketers will need to engage with smart devices and interfaces across the home. There is therefore the need to create unique experiences for their target consumers. These can be created through the following:

- *Content*: ensuring great experience with all e-mails and mobile apps.
- *Commerce*: ensuring that they harness not just the physical retail experience but also the e-commerce and/or a hybrid experience.
- *Community*: localising the experience and making use of virtual fairs or even webinars on home repair for consumers.

- *Convenience*: utilising loyalty programs to offer consumers benefits or price-offs.

Finally, the biggest topic that will need to be covered by academics is Cyber Security. There is a need to understand the privacy issues, legal issues, and data protection issues.

REFERENCES

McKinsey – *https://www.mckinsey.com/business-functions/marketing-and-sales/our-insights/reimagining-marketing-in-the-next-normal*

Harvard Business Review – *https://hbr.org/2021/03/10-truths-about-marketing-after-the-pandemic*

https://www.ey.com/en_au/consumer-products-retail/how-covid-19-could-change-consumer-behavior

Chapter

6

The Rise and Fall of Farming

Angus Hooke, Universal Business School Sydney

Greg Whateley, Universal Business School Sydney

Andrew West, Universal Business School Sydney

ABSTRACT

Throughout the Industrial Era (1800-2000), a major concern of economists was the conflict between the effects of continuing increases in population and income on the demand for food and the finite supply of arable land on the supply of food. Courses in Resource Economics highlighted the Malthusian model that preached abstinence and frugality but predicted famines and early deaths. However, since the 1960s the growth rate of population has declined, per capita consumption of food has reached saturation point for about 40% of the global population, and new technologies have led to excess supply and falling real prices in farm product markets, increasing poverty among farmers, and withdrawal of land from the farming sector. This chapter discusses the outlook for the farm products market during the remainder of the 21st century. It also shows how recent projections have been incorporated into an undergraduate course in Economics at a higher education provider in Sydney.

INTRODUCTION

Farming is a relatively new activity for humans. The main drivers of economic production and growth throughout most of human history (it is about 3 million years since Homo habilis emerged in the Rift Valley of Africa) have been foraging and scavenging (66%

of the time) and hunting (33%). It was not until the 100,000-year ice age ended about 15,000 years ago that farming emerged, slowly at first along the banks of the Euphrates and Tigris rivers in the Middle East, and then rapidly and often independently in virtually all parts of the globe apart from Australia. By the start of the Common Era (CE), more than half of the world's population was engaged in farming (Hooke, 2019).

Farming disrupted the economic and social lives of humans. People ceased to be members of small nomadic tribes, instead forming villages that grew into towns (the first town is believed to be Jericho, about 11,000 years ago), then cities (Uruk, around 7,000 years ago) and modern economies (Sumer, in what is now southern Iraq) about 6,000 years ago. During the Farming Era (10,000 BCE – CE 1800) population rose from 4 million to 900 million and per capita income tripled to I$250 (I$ is an international dollar – what a US dollar would buy in New York in July, in this chapter, of the year 2020). Total GWP in the 12 millennia of the Farming Era was about 60 times larger than that produced during the 3 million years of the preceding foraging, scavenging, and hunting eras.

Economics students require a strong foundation in economic principles and techniques that they can apply to the wide range of problems facing the world in the 21st century. Historical knowledge of global farm product markets provides context for an important area of resource economics and a basis for making projections of future performance in these markets. To take these economic principles, techniques, and knowledge and then critically analyse the logic, assumptions, evidence, and context presented are the corner stone of higher education built into course outcomes and graduate attributes. This is particularly the case in relation to food production as the basis of the first two goals (no poverty and zero hunger) of the United Nations Sustainable Development Goals (UN Department of Economic and Social Affairs, 2021).

PERFORMANCE OF THE FARM SECTOR, CE 1800-2000

In 1800, farm production (valued at the farmgate) accounted for around 80% of gross world product (GWP). While being replaced

by industry as the main engine of economic growth during the
Industrial Era (CE 1800-2000), farm production (gross agricultural
product - GAP) increased 26-fold, to I$5.6 trillion (Table 2). This
reflected a three-fold rise in land under farming, to 5,100 million
hectares (MHa), and a 10-fold increase in land productivity, to
almost I$1,100 per hectare. Nevertheless, much stronger growth of
production in the manufacturing and services sectors reduced the
farm sector's share in GWP to only 7.5% in 2000. On the
consumption side, global population rose six-fold during the Era,
to 6.1 billion, and per capita consumption of farm products
increased four-fold to I$911.

Table 2 - Total production (GWP) and agricultural production, 1800-2000 (Source:
FAO publications, World Factbook, Hooke (2021))

	1800	1850	1900	1950	2000	AAGR (%)
Production						
GWP (I$ b)	268	920	3,163	10,873	74,061	2.9
GAP (I$ b)	214	375	822	1,786	5,574	1.6
Land (MHa)	1,420	1,872	2,624	4,037	5,100	0.6
Productivity (I$/Ha)	151	200	313	443	1,093	1.0
GAP/GWP (%)	80.0	40.8	26.0	16.4	7.5	-1.2
Consumption						
Population (m)	990	1,260	1,650	2,540	6,120	0.9
PC Consumption (I$)	216	298	498	703	911	0.7

PROJECTIONS FOR THE FARM SECTOR DURING THE 21ST CENTURY

Demand for farm products

We now consider how the demand for farm (food) products might change during the first and second halves of the 21st century. While changes in consumption are not the same as changes in demand (the latter assume no change in price), the price elasticity of demand for farm products is close to zero for a large and increasing proportion of the world's population. (If people's desire for a product is satiated, reductions in price will not cause them to consume more.) With per capita real incomes in the developing countries expected to continue rising strongly, the growth rates of demand for, and consumption of, farm products are likely to merge as we progress through the 21st century.

We start with the identity that the demand for farm products (FD) is equal to the product of population (P) and average per capita demand for farm products (C). C is the sum of the per capita consumption of farm products among high-income consumers (CH) multiplied by the share of the high-income consumers in total population (PH / P) and the per capita consumption of farm products among lower-income consumers (CL) multiplied by the share of the lower-income consumers in total population (PL / P). Formally:

$$FD \quad = P * C \qquad\qquad (1)$$

$$C \quad = (CH * PH \, / \, P) + (CL * PL \, / \, P) \qquad\qquad (2)$$

For population, we adopt the 'median variant' projections made by the UN Population Division (UNPD). These assume that fertility rates across countries will tend to converge around the long-run, stable-population rate of 2.1 and that the mortality rate will continue to decline. UNDP projects that the AAGR of population, which peaked at 2.2% in the 1960s, will fall to 0.9% in 2001-50 and 0.2% in 2051-2100.

For consumers with per capita income above about I$20,000, the income elasticity of demand for farm products is close to zero. Consumers in this category comprise most of the population in the OECD countries and the middle-income and upper-income classes in the developing countries. It is estimated to have included about 40% of the global population in 2000. Publications by the United Nations' Food and Agriculture Organization (FAO) suggest that the per capita consumption of farm products of those in this category in 2000 was about I$1,050, implying that in the lower-income population it was I$820 (FAO, 2021). The 25% gap in per capita consumption between the high-income and the lower-income consumers is greater than the 10% difference in the calorie consumption of residents of high-income and lower-income countries (3,300 calories per day in the high-income countries – CPD – compared with 3,000 CPD in the lower-income countries) because of the higher share of more-expensive meat-sourced calories in the diets of those in the high-income countries. Based on projections of per capita income by Hooke & Alati (2021), it is assumed that the per capita consumption of farm products by lower-income consumers will increase to 95% of the level of high-income consumers in 2050 and to 100% by 2100.

Table 3 shows the forecasts for global food demand in 2050 and 2100. The AAGR of food demand, which was 1.6% during the Industrial Era, is projected to decline to 1.2% in 2001-50 and 0.3% in 2051-2000. The projection for 2001-50 is close to FAO's prediction of 1.1%. Accepting the forecasts for GWP in the 21st century by Hooke & Alati (2021), the projections for food demand/consumption imply that the share of the farm sector in GWP will fall to about 2% in 2050 and less than 1% in 2100. Farming will become a boutique activity.

Table 3 - Demand for Farm Products, 2021-2100 (Source. FAO publications, World Factbook, and projections by the authors)

	Values			AAGR (%)	
	2000	**2050**	**2100**	**2001-50**	**2051-2100**
Population (m)	6,120	9,740	10,880	0.9	0.2
PCC Ag (I$)	911	1,019	1,050	0.2	0.1
HI consumers	1,050	1,050	1,050	0.0	0.0
LI consumers	818	998	1,050	0.4	0.1
GAP (I$ b)	5,574	9,920	11,424	1.2	0.3
GWP (I$ b)	74,061	514,624	1,730,546	4.0	2.5
GAP/GWP (%)	7.5	1.9	0.7		

Supply of farm products

In contrast with the demand for farm products, the price elasticity of supply of farm products is quite high. Hence, changes in the real price of farm products will cause changes in the growth of supply to diverge from changes in the growth of production. Given the low price-elasticity of demand for farm products, any imbalances between changes in demand and supply will be corrected almost entirely by adjustments on the supply side.

Again, by definition, the quantity supplied of farm products at any given real price is the (mathematical) product of land under farming (L) and average land productivity (V). The growth of farm production (fS) is thus (approximately) equal to the growth of land under farming (l) plus the growth of land productivity (v). (On the de minimis principle, we neglect the third component, lv).

$$FS = L * V \qquad (3)$$

$$fS = l + v \qquad (4)$$

In the latter half of the 20th century, the AAGR of land productivity was 2.3%. Diamandis and Kotler (2012) have shown that land productivity is more than twice as high in the United States as in the rest of the world, mainly because US farmers use more and better inputs (machinery, irrigation, fertilisers, and pesticides) and employ better farm practices. However, the global phenomenon of converging resource inputs and management practices is not restricted to the manufacturing and services sectors. It is also occurring in farming. Continuation of convergence across countries would double land productivity; its continuation within countries would lead to a more-than doubling. By itself, convergence would lead to an AAGR for land productivity of about 1.5% during the first half of the 21st century.

Further, despite falling real prices and a generally unfavourable investment climate for farming, new and maturing technologies are promising substantial increases in land productivity among the productivity leaders. These include incremental technologies such as genetically modified plants (resulting in, for example, more, bigger, and tastier oranges per tree) and animals (e.g., more and richer milk per cow) and precision farming, which provides customised treatment to individual plants, allowing every plant to realise its optimum size, quality, and appearance potential. They also include radical technologies that reduce substantially the need for land, such as vertical farming, or even eliminate the need for land completely, such as 3D printing of meat and milk.

The area of the Earth's surface is approximately 51,000 MHa, of which 36,100 MHa (71%) is covered by oceans (Table 4). Almost a third of the land is uninhabitable. Habitable land is divided evenly between forests/shrubs (5,000 MHa) and human activities (5,250 MHa). The latter is almost entirely farming – land for urban purposes (such as houses, offices, factories, schools, roads, and sporting fields) account for only 3% of habitable land, 1% of global land, and 0.3% of the area of the Earth. Approximately 80% of farmland is used for pastoral activities (e.g., tending of cattle, pigs, sheep, goats, and chickens) and the remainder is used for cultivating crops (mainly wheat, soybeans, rice, fruits, and vegetables).

Table 4 - Global land use, 2000 (Source. FAO publications)

	MHa	% of Earth	% of Land
Earth	**51,000**	**100.0**	
Oceans	36,100	70.8	
Land	**14,900**	**29.2**	**100.0**
Uninhabitable	4,650	9.1	31.2
Deserts	2,900	5.7	19.5
Glaciers	1,600	3.1	10.7
Freshwater	150	0.3	1.0
Habitable	**10,250**	**20.1**	**68.8**
Forests & shrubs	5,000	9.8	33.6
Human activities	5,250	10.3	35.2
Urban	150	0.3	1.0
Farming	5,100	10.0	34.2
Crops	1,100	2.2	7.4
Livestock	4,000	7.8	26.8

The combination of convergence and incremental innovations should allow land productivity to maintain its late 20th century AAGR of 2.3% in the first half of the 21st century. This would halve the area of land under farming to 2,500 MHa in 2050. The projected increase in global population of 60% and a rise in the urbanisation ratio from 50% to 70% would increase the demand for urban land. However, urban development is not land-intensive, and the increase would be only 100 MH. For lack of any alternative use, the remaining 2,500 MHa released from farming would presumably be transformed into forests/shrubs, increasing the area under the latter to about 7,500 MHa, or about its level at the beginning of the Farming Era. More radical innovations, such as vertical farming and 3D printing of food, which (if not superseded) should be mature technologies by the second half of this century, would release most of the remaining farmland, allowing the area under forests to rise well above its pre-Farming era level.

CHANGES IN ECONOMICS COURSE

A course in Economics inherited by one of the authors included a 3-hour topic on Resource Economics. The theme of the topic was that increases in population and incomes are placing excessive demands on farmland, increasing food prices, and aggravating global poverty. It suggested that policies should focus on (1) reducing wastage (currently, 40% of farm production does not complete the journey "from the farm to the fork"), (2) increasing expenditure on research to raise land productivity, and (3) ensuring that more land is not allocated to golf courses and other (micro) land-intensive leisure pursuits.

The unit has been modified to describe, analyse, and evaluate the land-abundance as well as the land-scarcity scenario. Students work through mathematical models to derive the effects of the two scenarios on the dependent variables of food production, land required for farming, and global poverty. They then apply critical thinking techniques to assess the logic, assumptions, and evidence used in the models. Coursework provided online by the students after the class mostly contain the following conclusions: (1) Because the price elasticity of demand for farm products is very low compared to that of supply, reduction in wastage by high-income consumers would reduce production and the incomes of farmers, but have a negligible impact on food available to low-income consumers; (2) Again because of relative price elasticities, supporting new technologies that increase supply have the perverse effect of reducing price by a much greater percentage than they increase production. Since about 90% of the world's poor are farmers who earn most of their income from the sale of farm products but spend a vastly smaller proportion on buying farm products, measures that increase supply aggravate global poverty; (3) Doubling or tripling land area used for leisure activities would have a negligible impact on land available for farming (which, in any case, is not in short supply); and (4) Most of the land now used for farming will, for lack of any alternative use, revert to forests/shrubs during the present century.

REFERENCES

Diamandis, P. and Kotler, S. (2012. *Abundance: The Future is Better Than You Think*. Free Press.

FAO (2021). *How to feed the world in 2050*. Retrieved from *https://www.fao.org/fileadmin/templates/wsfs/docs/expert*

Hooke, A. (2019). *Global Economic Development: Past. Present, and Future*. Lakeland House.

Hooke, A. and Alati, L. (2021). *Technological Breakthroughs and Future Business Opportunities in Education, Health, and Outer Space*. IGI Global.

Johns Hopkins Center for a Liveable Future (2021*). History of Agriculture*. Retrieved from *https://www.foodsystemprimer.org/food-production/history-of-agriculture*

UN Department of Economic and Social Affairs (2021). *The 17 Goals*, Retrieved from *https://sdgs.un.org/goals*

Section 2:

Course Delivery

Chapter

7

Computerising Accounting Practice to Encourage Learning

Nilima Paul, Universal Business School Sydney

ABSTRACT

The invention and development of computing hardware and accounting software have transformed accounting practices. Processes that were performed manually in the latter part of the 20th century are now executed by computers using sophisticated accounting software packages. As a result, new graduates entering the accounting profession must not only possess a thorough knowledge of accounting principles and processes, they must also have strong computing skills. In this chapter, the author discusses how she introduced a sophisticated computer package into a postgraduate course in accounting and how combining this with an appropriate weight in assessments increased student motivation, participation, and performance.

INTRODUCTION

The history of accounting is thousands of years old. In 4000 BC, traders in Mesopotamia, home of the world's first documented civilisations and economies, were keeping records of transactions using clay tokens as symbols for objects and putting marks on them to denote their number. Later, these and other details were recorded on papyrus, and then on paper.

The concept of double-entry book-keeping was documented in 1494 by Luca Pacioli, a housemate of Leonardo da Vinci and widely recognized as the 'Father of Accounting and Bookkeeping'. Pacioli included a description of this golden rule, which was being practiced in parts of Italy, in Chapter 5 of his mathematics book *Summa de Scriputa.*

Accounting has three beautiful qualities: (1) The recording of financial transactions is the same in virtually all businesses around the world; (2) Generally Accepted Accounting Principles (GAAP) have been widely adopted across businesses; and (3) All humans deal with accounting concepts in their daily lives. For example, suppose that I am a student at UBSS (Universal Business School Sydney). I am sitting in a class because of a business transaction. I have two changes and UBSS has two changes. My changes are: (1) I paid tuition fees and (2) I am receiving an education service. Similarly, UBSS has two changes: (1) UBSS received money from me and (2) UBSS is providing the education service to me.

The introduction of technology has changed enormously the role of modern professional accountants. Most repetitive accounting tasks are now computerised; accountants can rely on spreadsheets and software packages for much of their daily work. Information technology has enabled businesses to develop and use computerised systems to record, process, and store important details of financial transactions.

RATIONALE

Modern professional accountants use a wide range of computer applications to assist them in their daily work. They use email to communicate, search engines to undertake research, and accounting software to record and analyse financial transactions for business decision-making. Computerised accounting systems have replaced manual accounting systems in most organisations throughout the world. Technological advancements help accountants keep accurate records of business transactions. Technology has provided the accounting industry with new avenues to explore, create new products and services, and enable its professionals to gain new skills and take on additional responsibilities.

Today, accounting is cloud-based. COVID-19 completely changed the business landscape. Cloud-based accounting came to the forefront, with a wide range of benefits for business: it is online; it is secure; and users can easily and quickly access their management systems, core financial data, and inventory systems to ensure their business runs smoothly during this turbulent time. Cloud-based accounting has allowed accountants to be mobile and reactive to the needs of their clients. Importantly, it has also put businesses in touch with clients that are not just around the corner but are far away, across the globe. Continuing professional development and education in this area will be necessary for accountants.

Moreover, the development of sophisticated accounting software enhances accountants' mobile capabilities. Wherever they are, accountants can use their smartphones to provide quotes, generate invoices, reconcile bank statements, pay bills, analyse business operations, and ensure that wages are paid on time. An understanding of accounting software and other business and financial models will be necessary if practicing accountants are to prepare financial statements in an effective and timely manner and to discharge their responsibilities properly.

At UBSS, MBA accounting students are increasingly being exposed to the benefits of computerised accounting. Computerised accounting packages are being included in material being presented in class and assessments are being updated to reward students who use these packages.

REALITY

This chapter explains the impact that introducing an accounting software package (MYOB) to the subject **Accounting Systems and Processes** has had on students' acquisition of practical accounting knowledge. Today's accountants use a wide range of computer applications to perform routine tasks in the workplace. They use accounting software to record, analyse, and process financial information needed for business decision making. Computerised accounting systems now play a vital role in communicating business financial reports to known and unknown users. At UBSS, MBA accounting students are encouraged to practice computerised accounting to better prepare them for their future careers.

In 2018, the unit **Accounting Systems and Processes** was introduced in the MBA program. It had four assessments: Test 1: 15%, Test 2: 15%, Group presentation 20%, and Final exam 50%. Under this assessment allocation, students had little engagement with computerised accounting. At that time, students learnt mainly manual accounting. As computerised accounting has considerable benefits for students seeking to enter and succeed in the Australian job market, MYOB was added in 2019, and the assessment allocation was changed to Test 15%, Computerised accounting practice 25%, and Final exam 60%. The explicit and relatively high share of the new module in overall assessment was aimed at giving students more motivation to learn computerised accounting systems. The author's observation is that before introducing MYOB, student attendance in classes was relatively low. After introducing the package, student attendance was relatively high. This is reflected in students' anonymous feedback after completing the unit, which is also shown in unit results (Table 5). Table 6 (after References) 1 provides further anonymous student feedback, which was sent by email (Trimester 2, 2021).

Table 5 - Percentage Grades Distribution Pre- & Post-MYOB

Period	Grades Distribution					
	AF	**F**	**P**	**C**	**D**	**HD**
Pre-MYOB						
16/01/2017	18	6	13	16	28	19
8/05/2017	10	10	20	30	10	20
28/08/2017	12	4	17	25	29	13
15/01/2018	8			16	64	12
7/05/2018		5	13	41	25	16
27/08/2018	12	24	22	15	18	9
Average	*10*	*8*	*14*	*24*	*29*	*15*

Period	Grades Distribution					
	AF	**F**	**P**	**C**	**D**	**HD**
Post-MYOB						
21/01/2019	16	16	28	14	16	10
13/05/2019	21	16	31	17	12	3
9/02/2019	19	21	24	17	17	2
20/01/2020	6	8	25	31	19	11
11/05/2020	18	8	23	22	21	8
31/08/2020	17	10	25	22	21	5
11/01/2021	17	12	29	22	11	9
3/05/2021	21	11	23	20	22	3
Average	*17*	*13*	*26*	*21*	*17*	*6*

Key: AF - Absent Fail, F - Fail, P - Pass, C - Credit,
D - Distinction, HD - High Distinction.

Data source: UBSS Management (GCA).

The results suggest that students' performance over the trimesters has improved, including when the shares of Fail and Pass, and Fail-to-Credit, Distinction and High Distinction are considered. Figure 8 shows this relationship through the trends. However, while the percentage of Fail grades has declined with the introduction of MYOB and the percentage of Passes has increased, the percentages of other favourable results (Credit, Distinction and High Distinction combined) has declined. It is important to note that a student's top priority is to achieve at least a Pass, and that attaining a Credit or higher grade is a secondary (though for some, still a very important) objective. It seems that the introduction of MYOB has inspired weaker students to become more involved in their studies and this has led to a better outcome in the form of a higher percentage passing the exams.

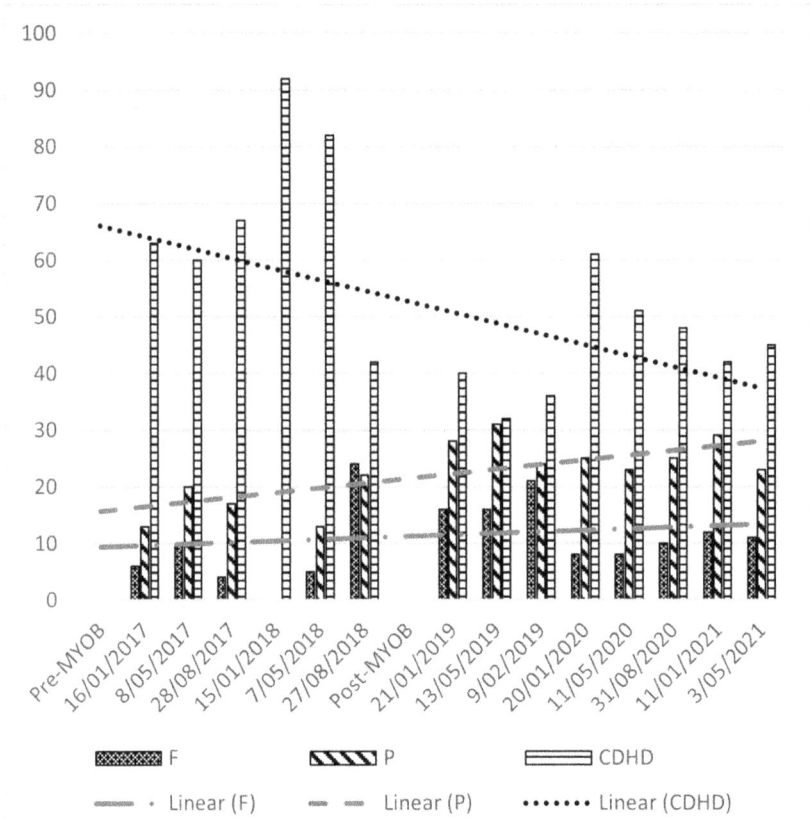

Figure 8 - Chart Showing Trends in the Results Pre- & Post MYOB

Data source: UBSS Management (GCA)

Students' feedback (Table 6 - below) indicates that the inclusion of computerised accounting and giving it a high weight in the assessment for the subject has had a highly positive impact on both the learning of students and their keenness to work in the accounting profession. This suggests that computerised accounting can be effectively utilised and integrated in class to improve students learning of accounting. Studying manual accounting systems is still required because of the greater depth of understanding gained by going through each step in the documentation and recording of individual business transactions, but computerised accounting increases student knowledge, skills, job-readiness, and confidence.

THE FUTURE

The author's experience with introducing MYOB into **Accounting Systems and Processes** suggests that student learning outcomes might be improved by the inclusion of computerised accounting modules in other subjects. For example, the software "Active Data Excel" could be offered in the unit **Auditing**, and the software "MS Visio" could be added to the subject, **Accounting Information Systems**.

CONCLUSIONS

Teaching and learning are two-way communication processes that require active participation by both teachers and students. Effective implementation of computerised accounting in subjects motivates students to play a more active role in the learning process, and this can assist them to better understand subject matter by doing what will be required of them in the real world. Computerised accounting provides considerable benefits for students. It allows them to apply the knowledge they have gained in class and therefore accelerates the learning process. Using accounting software in a subject provides a more accurate reflection of industry practice, which may better prepare students for the challenging contemporary business world and the ever-changing accounting profession. Undertaking practical exercises in computerised accounting can provide valuable learning experiences for students. These active learning experiences can significantly enhance student learning.

REFERENCES

Abed, S. 2014. *A review of e-accounting education for undergraduate accounting degrees.* Int. Bus. Res., 7: 113-119.

Ballard, B. and Chandry, J. (1991). *Teaching Students from Overseas: A Brief Guide for Lecturers and Supervisors,* Longman Cheshire, Sydney.

Boyce, G. (1999). *Computer-assisted teaching and learning in accounting: pedagogy or product?,* Journal of Accounting Education, Vol. 17 Nos 2/3, pp. 191-220.

McDowall, T. and Jackling, B. (2006). *The impact of computer-assisted learning on academic grades: an assessment of students' perceptions,* Accounting Education: An International Journal, Vol. 15 No. 4, pp. 377-389.

Table 6 - Anonymous student feedback sent by email (T2, 2021)

Ref #	Feedback
1	"MYOB really help me to learn more about accounting system. It gave me more confident to work in field".
2	"MYOB Practice Set was useful to let me get familiar with the whole accounting process from setting up the company file. I think this MYOB Practice is necessary as I have a better understanding of the accounting process".
3	"I think MYOB is a good pace setter interns of preparing student for the outside-class world, the professional arena. It gives a good insight of what to expect and a golden chance to interact with a global too that we might interact with when we go out there. Overall, MYOB is helpful for accounting students".
4	"MYOB was useful tool in accounting system as it offers different Software and tools that provide good features to work online, manage invoices, calculate GST, sell item and service. It saves time and make things easier and it also Improving the speed and accuracy of accounting task. I found this very useful".

Ref #	Feedback
5	"MYOB was helpful for me to learn the computer skill and how to make entries on computer and how to record the different entries and in starting I feel little difficult but in later find it was very interesting to learn computer skill and the MYOB is very helpful in subject as well".
6	"I have learnt MYOB software in your class, and I think this software is useful, and help me understand the accounting well. As the same time, it would be great to have more practice in the class".
7	"I learned a lot from the software MYOB, and it is practical and useful for my future career. It helps me to understand the accounting process".
8	"MYOB was Useful that, it helps me in accounting".
9	"MYOB was very helpful, and I am working with tax consultants and the practice of MYOB is helping me in my job also".
10	"My experience regarding MYOB was excellent and learned a lot about that....it was very great".
11	"In my view MYOB project was very helpful as it gives real work experience. I learned a lot by putting my learning into practice".
12	"It was very interesting and useful".
13	"MYOB is fantastic it is very helpful in learning, and it will help me in my future accounting career".
14	"I learn more about bookkeeping and accounting by practising MYOB".

Chapter

8

Enhancing Student Engagement? Let's Get Real!

Syed Uddin, Universal Business School Sydney

ABSTRACT

Achieving the engagement of learners is a challenging task. The challenge is especially daunting when lessons are delivered online. Devising mitigating strategies requires a clear understanding of the ground realities. An attempt has been made in this chapter to explore the issue of learners' engagement. Since the onset of the COVID-19 pandemic and the switch to online learning, international students in non-university settings appear to have been less engaged for various reasons, and some of those reasons seem easier to manage than others. To prevent the effectiveness and sustainability of academic programs from being unintended casualties of the move to online learning, complacency should not be an option.

INTRODUCTION

Engagement is the *'sine qua non'* of effective learning. It sharpens learners' attention, motivates them to apply higher-level critical thinking, and promotes meaningful learning experiences. The effectiveness and long-term sustainability of academic programs depend on real engagement - which is much more than a mere 'checklist' ticking exercise. Thus 'engagement' continues to attract the attention of academics, educational strategists, and policy makers.

OBJECTIVES AND RATIONALE

The importance of learner engagement in higher education is being increasingly recognised. But how to inspire learners best is still a matter of debate. At a time when face-to-face teaching has been sidelined in favour of virtual delivery, the issue of students' engagement is more important than ever. Below, the author uses insights derived from a case study he conducted to explore this issue in some detail. Aspects like what it really means to be engaged, what could be the reasons for engagement/disengagement, and what it takes to achieve better engagement are all explored. Students, both current and prospective, will be the ultimate beneficiaries of this effort as it is primarily directed towards enhancing students' overall learning experiences. Policy makers, academic administrators, researchers, and members of the teaching fraternity will also benefit from this 'front-line' version of the ground realities. This effort, however, should not be considered as a 'cure-all' remedy due to its limited scope.

DECIPHERING ENGAGEMENT/ DISENGAGEMENT

Engagement provides value for all. It is "an important prerequisite for improving student achievement and student experience" and it can be considered "an indicator of institutional success" (Baron and Corbin, 2012, p.759). According to Bowen (2005, pp. 4-7) educational engagement can happen in four different ways, namely student engagement: with the *learning process* i.e., active involvement.; with an *object of study* i.e., transformative in some way; with contexts of the subject of study i.e., multi-disciplinary or inter-disciplinary learning; and finally, with the *human condition* i.e., learning in civic and cultural contexts. Many researchers (Zhao et al., 2021, p.2) are of the opinion that students' perceptions of the learning environment play a vital role in their 'skill development'. Enhancement of academic achievement depends on the learning environment where students enjoy freedom, their skills development is promoted based on the curriculum and instruction, and enjoyable interpersonal relationships are nurtured (Deci &

Ryan, 1985; Reeve, 2002; Ryan & Deci, 2000). A major US study (2017) highlighted 'higher order learning (curriculum leaning) and effective teaching practices (delivery leaning)' as being important engagement indicators.

International post-graduate students taking business courses with private partner providers (outreach campuses run by private partners under twinning arrangements with universities) have been found to be less engaged for various reasons (Uddin, 2015). Since the student cohorts at stand-alone private higher education providers are similar in almost all respects to those of students attending university outreach partner providers' programs, the nature and extent of disengagement are unlikely to be substantially different for these students. Based on a case-study type, small-scale semi-purposive survey (Uddin, 2015) and students' spontaneous feedback (Ng, 2021) received personally from time to time, coupled with a prolonged experience in dealing with international students, the author of this chapter is well-placed to identify some of the reasons for students' disengagement. It is to be noted here that these reasons may not be applicable to all international students, nor to all study programs in all locations. The reasons are discussed under four headings:

Content leaning

- Outdated material
- Does not provoke challenge or creativity
- No flexibility in terms of choice of subjects/units

Delivery leaning

- Complacency
- Monotonous delivery – does not ignite passion
- Ineffective interaction
- Cultural insensitivity and lack of empathy

Learner leaning

- Entitlement mentality - schools exist to provide diplomas and degrees
- Lack of intrinsic motivation - enrolling into programs out of necessity rather than desire
- Juggling irreconcilable demands
- Anchoring priorities somewhere other than in the study program

Context leaning

- Wider gap between students' expectations and ground realities re physical facilities and resources (library, sports, clubs etc.)
- Volatility of income
- Bleak prospects regarding qualifying for Australian residency
- Slim chances of embarking on a professional career

A quick browse through the above-mentioned reasons will force even a casual observer to the conclusion that 'engagement' is a multi-party and multifaceted phenomenon, and that no one person could possibly do all the heavy lifting to facilitate it. The 'content' and the 'delivery' leaning issues appear to be more manageable than the issues relating to the 'learner' and the learning 'context'.

THE WAY FORWARD

Engaged teaching (Karasik, 2012 p.121) has been compared with 'salesmanship - you have to get the buyer's attention before you can make a sale'. Karasik (2012, pp.121-128) proposed some simple rules in this regard, including 'knowing the audience, being really there, making it personal in a professional way, treating them as individuals, using humour and keeping current and relevant'. Some authors view student engagement as a 'shared responsibility" (Zepke, Leach & Butler, 2014 p.395). Some believe (Cook-Sather & Luz, 2015) that a re-defined learners' role (where faculty and learners have some sort of partnership) might be the way forward.

Learner engagement is better when learners are provided with control over the content, the sequence, and the pace of delivery; and when learners can practice the content and receive feedback. These features are likely to enhance the meaningfulness of learning and stimulate students' desire to learn. Blended learning has been considered as more engaging for learners because the on-line learning component allows them to control the learning process (i.e., to review and skip content) and provides them with a relatively care-free and safe environment in which they feel free to make errors (Noe, Tews, & Dachner, 2010). Authors like Kolb & Kolb, (2010) believe that a supportive environment as well as challenging opportunities for repetitive practice are conducive to better learning and would improve learners' intrinsic motivation to play, learn, and experiment. Ayelet Israeli's (2020) REMOTE framework (Reactions, Eye contact, Manageable, Organized, Thoughtful, and Engagement & evaluation) is quite helpful in this regard.

Replication of techniques that are effective in face-to-face teaching is not always possible with online delivery because students are not physically visible and are often unwilling to turn their cameras on. This has been considered by some (Tse, 2021, p. 98) as a 'worrying trend'. So, an outright and complete turnaround regarding the issues standing in the way of learners' engagement in online delivery is not a realistic proposition. The situation, however, could be improved with the right strategies. Issues relating to 'content' and 'delivery' could be better managed with the help of carefully chosen relevant materials, orderly delivery, explanations with current, familiar, and illustrative examples, thought-provoking activities requiring critical thinking, problem-solving focused discussion, and the use of humour and anecdotes. Establishing ongoing rapport with the students alongside timely developmental feedback on their work are also helpful. If students (can be convinced/required to) keep their video cameras on while online, some difficulties can be better managed. Similar efforts in the US were found to enhance teaching effectiveness and promote student comprehension and learning (National Survey of Student Engagement, 2017).

The option 'to choose units and programs from among a pool of available choices' is not practicable for many private providers due to budgetary and capacity constraints. For the same reason, providing 'sport and physical library facilities' may not be a viable option either. E-libraries are minimising this void to some extent. An attitudinal change with a degree of cross-cultural literacy among the teaching staff can smooth-out the 'rough' edges. Using a respectful tone and authentic delivery are likely to augment quality participation as really thirsty learners do not respond well when there is insincerity - whether perceived or real. A carefully crafted passionate appeal and the tactics of ingratiation might also work to an extent.

As far as 'learners and the context' related issues are concerned, the options appear quite limited. The macroeconomic and demographic priorities and the policies of the Australian government seem to be having negative and cascading effects on learners' motivation. It is an open secret that the possibility of gaining residency used to be the most important determinant of learners' choice of units and educational programs. The degree of involvement with the program and the level of motivation were correlated with the likelihood of gaining residency. With online or face-to-face learning, now the prospect of gaining residency is almost non-existent, and the obvious casualty is intrinsic motivation.

With the help of exciting initiatives, like inviting carefully selected students to have a one-on-one dialogue with the senior academic leadership/adjunct faculties with substantial industry exposure broadcasted via YouTube, a positive gradual shift in attitude may be possible. Well-coordinated and concerted efforts among the agents supplying students, marketing teams, overseas liaison offices, academic support services, academic administrators, and faculty staff might help to gradually shape learners' thinking and behaviour. Aspects relating to perceived 'bleak prospects' by students are unlikely to be resolved at the institutional level as these are macro dimensions requiring the highest level (governmental) policy interventions. A quick fix is therefore not an option here. With COVID-19 keeping all deliveries online, some of the actions described above will be difficult to ensure in the short run (Uddin, 2021).

Under these circumstances, it is logical to think that one strategy will not work for everyone. The strategies might need some adjustment depending on, among other factors, the background of the students being taught. Any generalisation that the learners from a particular geographic region are mostly identical regarding educational expectations and experiences may not deliver the desired outcomes in terms of student engagement and learning enhancement. For example, students from the Indian sub-continent are different in terms of language proficiency, attitudes and expectations compared to students from East Asian countries. It is, thus, quite naive to assume that 'one size fits all' when it comes to catering for international students. Moreover, students with an Asian background were found (Chavan, 2011) to have different learning styles to other students. Since no two individuals are alike, it is very unlikely that there would be 'one best way' to deal with everyone (Robbins et al., 2016).

CONCLUSIONS

For effective engagement of international students, one might have to look at several things. These include the context in which the learning is taking place, the materials that are being used, the learners' ability, the facilitator's expertise and enthusiasm, the reasons for learning, the atmosphere of learning, and the right approaches to take. Teaching techniques and styles also need to be suitable for the specific cohorts of learners considering their background and expectations. Just-about-right strategies coupled with a favourable atmosphere by taking the steps mentioned above are likely to improve students' engagement.

Due to its limited scope, this chapter could not cover all aspects, could not resolve all issues, and could not answer all questions concerning students' disengagement and remedies. Nevertheless, it has sown the seeds for a serious conversation about these subjects. To be of real value, and for all practical purposes, a longitudinal study would be worth contemplating at some stage in the near future. If, despite its limitations, this chapter has shed some light on the problems associated with student engagement, it will have achieved its purpose!

Complacency, or a 'do nothing' mindset, have the potential to alienate the most strategic stakeholders i.e., the international students, which in turn might rattle the foundations of learning and teaching. Therefore, an engaged teaching and learning environment is in the interest of everyone engaged in higher education.

REFERENCES

Baron, P. & Corbin, L. (2012). *Student engagement: rhetoric and reality.* Higher Education Research & Development, 31 (6), 759-772.

Bowen, S. (2005). *Engaged learning: Are we on the same page?* Peer Review, 7 (2), 4–7.

Chavan, M. (2011). *Higher Education Students' Attitudes Towards Experiential Learning in International Business.* Journal of Teaching in International Business, 22, 126–143.

Cook-Sather, A. and Luz, A. (2015). *Greater engagement in and responsibility for learning: what happens when students cross the threshold of student–faculty partnership.* Higher Education Research & Development, 34(6), 1097-1109.

Deci, E. L., & Ryan, R. M. (1985). *Intrinsic motivation and self-determination in human behaviour.* USA: Plenum Press.

Israeli, A. (2020). *Digital learning REMOTE a framework for teaching online.* Harvard Business Publishing accessed on 28 February 2021 from *https://hbsp.harvard.edu/inspiring-minds/remote-a-framework-for-teaching-online*

Karasik, R. J. (2012). *Engaged Teaching for Engaged Learning: Sharing Your Passion for Gerontology and Geriatrics,* Gerontology & Geriatrics Education. 33:2, 119-132.

Kolb, A. Y. & Kolb, D. A. (2010). *Learning to play, playing to learn: A case study of a ludic learning space.* Journal of Organizational Change Management, 23(1), 26-50.

National Survey of Student Engagement. (2017). *https://bit.ly/2Kyxkzo*

Ng, S. (2021). *Transitioning towards studying online: A reflection. An unpublished write-up by a current post graduate student studying with a private provider in Sydney*, 1-8. Australia.

Noe, R. A., Tews, M. J. and Dachner, A. M. (2010). *Learner Engagement: A New Perspective for Enhancing Our Understanding of Learner Motivation and Workplace Learning.* The Academy of Management Annals, 4(1), 279–315.

Reeve, J. (2002). *Self-determination theory applied to educational settings.* In E. L. Deci & R. M. Ryan (Eds.), Handbook of self-determination research, 183–203. NY, USA: University of Rochester Press.

Ryan, R. M., & Deci, E. L. (2000). *Self-determination theory and the facilitation of intrinsic motivation, social development, and well-being.* American Psychologist, 55 (1), 68–78. *https://doi.org/10.1037/0003-066X.55.1.68*

Robbins, S. P., Judge, T., Millett, B. and Boyle, M. (2016). *Organisational behaviour,* 17th edn, USA: Pearson.

Tse, H. (2021). *Plugged in But Disconnected: Challenges in the 2020 Online Transition.* Transitioning to Online Learning During Covid-19 Reflections by Practitioners. Edited by A. Hooke and G. Whateley. Sydney, Australia: Group Colleges Australia Pty Ltd, 95-99. ISBN 978-1-907453-30-4

Uddin, S. J. (2015). *Disengaged international students.* Negotiated Task submitted to Federation University for the partial fulfilment of Graduate Certificate in Higher Education qualification, 1-7.

Uddin, S. J. (2021). *Covid Driven Transition to Online Teaching: A Reflection. Transitioning to Online Learning During Covid-19 Reflections by Practitioners.* Edited by A. Hooke and G. Whateley. Sydney, Australia: Group Colleges Australia Pty Ltd, 43-48. ISBN 978-1-907453-30-4

Zepke, N., Leach, L. & Butler, P. (2014). *Student engagement: students' and teachers' perceptions.* Higher Education Research & Development, 33(2), 386-398.

Zhao, Y., Lin, S., Liu, J., Zhang, J., & Yu, Q. (2021). *Learning contextual factors, student engagement, and problem-solving skills: A Chinese perspective.* Social Behavior and Personality, 49(2), e 9796, https://doi.org/10.2224/sbp.9796, www.sbp-journal.com, 1-18.

Chapter

9

Using Vodcasts to Enhance Learning in a Postgraduate Economics Subject

Harry Tse, Universal Business School Sydney

ABSTRACT

For many years educators have sought to integrate videos into their pedagogical practices. To support 'blended learning - a thoughtful fusion of face-to-face and online learning experiences' (Garrison & Vaughn, 2008), the author developed a package of five-minute videos (called 'vodcasts') and used them in a postgraduate economics subject. The vodcasts were designed to introduce key economic concepts to students as a precursor and complement to face-to-face teaching. They were intended to be a flexible resource that addressed student diversity and helped students transition from undergraduate to postgraduate study. This chapter discusses the evolution of the project and the effects on student learning. Surveys and focus groups indicate that student perceptions of the vodcasts were resoundingly positive.

INTRODUCTION

Encouraging students to undertake prior activities so they are better prepared for new content delivered in class is not easy. This chapter describes a project undertaken to help students ease into an Economics subject by introducing a series of '5-minute, pre-class videos' (referred to as vodcasts). The vodcasts were 'flipped' and 'posted' on the Learning Management System so that students could watch them before attending class. Also, and perhaps more important, students could re-watch them as needed throughout the semester.

Blended learning allows students to undertake online learning of new material that is later integrated into classroom experiences. By engaging with vodcasts, students can acquire an early awareness of the basic concepts of a subject/topic and can 'tune in' for the upcoming face-to-face lectures.

MOTIVATIONS

The transition from undergraduate to postgraduate study can be difficult for students. It is especially hard if their introduction to postgraduate study includes an Economics subject that is a core part of the postgraduate business program. This is the situation faced by students the author teaches at Universal Business School Sydney (UBSS). The subject, Introductory Economics, covers the fundamental concepts, relationships, and theories of macro and micro economics. Not only is this subject often the first exposure students have to economic terminology and abstract concepts, many students also have English as their second language (ESL) and have been out of the university system for some time. In addition, most of the students are usually time poor. Finding a good balance between work, study, family commitments, and social life is a major challenge for them.

Like most introductory subjects, Economics involves sequential learning (Ritter, 2007). Each week's new material is built on the concepts and relationships covered in preceding lectures. Learners can quickly fall behind if they are not on top of each week's new material. Providing "flipped" (Abeysekera and Dawson, 2015) '5-minute, pre-class videos' before face-to-face learning and blending these into the syllabus can increase student engagement – particularly with a new subject.

Having a sound understanding of basic economic concepts is essential for mastering the more advanced subjects in the UBSS postgraduate program such as Business Finance, Accounting, Management, and Marketing. Business Finance is essentially applied economics because one needs to understand the principles of macroeconomics to follow the financial markets, while Accounting is about economic reporting. Introductory Economics covers the different types of market structure that students refer to when putting together marketing, strategic, or business plans in later subjects. As for Management subjects, students must apply basic economic quantitative techniques to derive and interpret results when analysing business performance.

BENEFITS OF 'FLIPPED' VIDEOS IN THE BUSINESS PROGRAM

Research shows that prior provision of appropriate digital resources can help students become familiar with key concepts before they are explained and expanded upon in class. The flipped classroom can increase student engagement (Smallhorn, 2017). Price and Walker (2019) suggest that the flexible delivery of videos allows learners to access material in their own time and at their own pace and facilitates the transition to postgraduate study of students from diverse backgrounds. New learners usually find abstract economic concepts challenging. The flipped videos provide clear and concise summaries of the topics before students come to class. The ability to rewind and adjust the playback speed of the vodcasts is especially helpful to ESL and time-poor students.

PRODUCTION OF THE VODCASTS

The inspiration for the vodcast project came from a one-day workshop entitled 'The Power of Screen Presenting'. That workshop convinced the author that vodcasts would be a useful vehicle for introducing and reinforcing fundamental economic concepts to students. Because of their 'flipped' and 'flexible' nature, vodcasts would be particularly helpful to linguistically and culturally diverse cohorts.

Before developing transcripts for the videos, the author collected and collated comments and suggestions from other teaching staff. A presenter was engaged to record the material on camera, and a special arrangement was made with the video-production crew to ensure their continuous support and guidance. To encourage students to watch the vodcasts before class, the content of the videos was incorporated into the tutorial exercises and assessments.

DISCUSSIONS OF RESULTS & FINDINGS

To measure the effects of the vodcasts on student performance, a Two-Sample Assuming Unequal Variances t-Test (Aspin-Welch-Satterthwaite test) was conducted between the control group of 335 students who undertook the subject in 2019 prior to the introduction of vodcasts and the sample group of 272 students who had access to the vodcasts in 2020.

In 2019, before the introduction of vodcasts, the average mark of students taking the Introductory Economics subject was 68.37. In 2020, when the vodcasts were used, it was 66.13 (Table 7). The difference in the mean, of -2.24, is statistically significant at the 2% level. However, one should not be overly concerned that the introduction of vodcasts was associated with a negative impact on final marks because previous research has shown that students' overall performance in Introductory Economics is influenced considerably by the levels of Mathematics and Economics taken prior to taking up the subject (Mallik 2016), and these differ significantly among cohorts.

Table 7 - Two-Sample Assuming Unequal Variances t-test results

	2019	2020
Mean	68.37104	66.12875
Variance	135.4486	129.6172
Observations	335	272
Hypothesized Mean Difference	0	
df	585	
t Stat	2.389122	
P(T<=t) one-tail	0.008602	
t Critical one-tail	1.647463	
P(T<=t) two-tail	0.017205	
t Critical two-tail	1.964027	

The grade comparison (Table 8 and Figure 9) indicates slight declines in the number of students achieving High Distinction (HD) and Distinction (D). The drop in the HD grade is not a major concern because HDs are only awarded to outstanding students whose performance is determined mainly by their intrinsic ability and motivation rather than by teaching quality, and these characteristics that differ considerably from cohort to cohort.

Table 8 - Grade comparison before and after the introduction of Vodcast

	Fail (%)	Pass (%)	Credit (%)	D (%)	HD (%)
Before (2019)	7.00	26.24	33.82	24.49	8.45
After (2020)	6.62	30.15	36.40	23.16	3.68

However, the improved performances of average students and those who are struggling were encouraging. There was a drop in the Fail grade from 7.00% to 6.62%, an improvement of 0.38 percentage point (pp). The Pass grade increased from 26.24% to 30.15%, a boost of 3.91pp. The Credit grade also rose, from 33.82% to 36.40%, an improvement of 2.58pp. These results suggest that the introduction of '5-minute, pre-class videos' helped average and below-average students achieve better results. The flipped classroom and blended learning approaches were useful for most students.

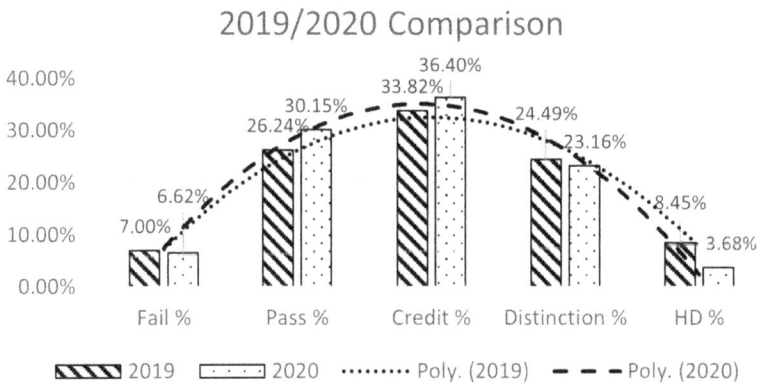

Figure 9 - Grade comparison before and after the introduction of Vodcast

KEY FINDINGS AND STUDENT COMMENTS FROM FOCUS GROUPS

The student feedback survey (SFU) results and colleague feedback showed a strong and positive indication that the vodcasts helped ease students' transition to postgraduate study and increased their engagement. Post-semester/trimester surveys were encouraging, with 62% of respondents indicating that the vodcasts addressed the subject topics at an adequate depth. Feedback from a colleague and student focus group interviews include such comments as:

> *"Harry's vodcasts provide a brief and clear summary of the main concepts to be considered in each lecture".* **Peter Docherty, Associate Professor, Economics Discipline Group, University of Technology Sydney.**

> *"I really enjoy them – it showed me the main idea and allowed me to understand a few more things that happened in class – so I could talk to myself and ask myself 'ok what's the key point – how can I better understand the theory?' ".*

> *"I watched the first ones as economics is totally new for me, I've never studied it before. That was really good and helped me feel prepared coming to class and feel that I understood a little more".*

CONCLUSION

There are many benefits from using flipped and blended learning vodcasts in terms of improving student engagement and easing the transition to postgraduate study. As a teaching and learning resource, vodcasts are an excellent introduction and revision tool as learners can watch them as many times as required (Ng 2015). Vodcasts are particularly useful for introducing fundamental economic concepts, allowing learners to come to class better prepared to take on more challenging theories and problem-solving exercises.

Vodcasts, however, have limitations as they are expensive and time consuming to produce. Educators and university managers should design syllabi in a way that supports the use of vodcasts as complements to in-class learning activities and experiences.

REFERENCES

Abeysekera, L. and Dawan P. (2015), *Motivation and cognitive load in the flipped classroom: definition, rational and a call for research*, Higher Education Research & Development 34(1): 1-14.

Garrison, D.R. & Vaughan, N.D. (2008), *Blended Learning in Higher Education: Framework, Principles, and guidelines.* San Francisco: Jossey-Bass.

Mallik, G., & Shankar, S. (2016). *Does prior knowledge of economics and higher level mathematics improve student learning in principles of economics,* Economic Analysis and Policy, Volume 49, March 2016, Pages 66-73.

Ng. W., (2015). *New Digital Technology in Education: Conceptualising Professional Learning for Educators.* Springer International Publishing.

Price, C., & Walker, M. (2019). *Improving the accessibility of foundation statistics for undergraduate business and management students using a flipped classroom.* Studies in Higher Education, DOI: 10.1080/03075079.2019. 1628204.

Ritter F. E.; et al., eds. (2007). *In order to learn: how the sequence of topics influences learning. Oxford series on cognitive models and architectures.* Oxford/New York: Oxford University Press. ISBN 978-0-19-517884-5.

Smallhorn, M. (2017). *The flipped classroom: A learning model to increase student engagement not academic achievement.* Student Success, B (2), 43-53. DOI: 10.5204/ssj. v8i2.381.

Two-Sample T-Tests Allowing Unequal Variance. Retrieved from *https://ncss-wpengine.netdna-ssl.com/wp-content/themes/ncss/pdf/Procedures/PASS/Two-Sample_T-Tests_Allowing_Unequal_Variance*

Chapter

10

Using a Marketing Perspective to Improve Learning

Ajay Kumar, Universal Business School Sydney

ABSTRACT

The traditional mode of delivering tertiary education has focused on face-to-face classes delivered to increasingly diverse global student cohorts. COVID-19 forced most providers to move abruptly to online delivery and, in countries exporting education, to smaller cohorts as international borders were closed. The author of this chapter argues that online delivery is here to stay, and that providers should learn from marketers how to make their product more attractive to students in order succeed in a more competitive education environment.

INTRODUCTION

The tertiary education industry is experiencing considerable change. Higher education providers in leading exporting countries such as the United States and Australia are catering to more socially and culturally diverse student populations than ever before, due largely to increasing numbers of foreign students (Jude & Ryan, 2005). In addition, the COVID–19 pandemic and the ensuing lockdowns forced most providers to (temporarily at least) abandon face–to-face (F2F) classes in favour of wholly online delivery. However, as is often the case, the recent, abrupt changes bring not only new challenges but also new opportunities.

These new opportunities require moving from the traditional strategy of sage-on-the-stage, F2F delivery to a more engaging online strategy that enhances the student learning experience. Lecturers, the most visible stakeholders in universities, have a key role to play. They need to redesign resources and delivery strategies to engage students who are now mostly millennials (born between 1981 and 1996 and so comfortable with online technologies) or members of generation Z (born after 1996, and so have never been offline). Lecturers also often play the role of customer service staff as most of the time they are the most frequent point of contact with students.

The diverse cultural backgrounds, different education experiences, and wide age range of globally sourced students may create emotional barriers between lectures and students, (Yahanpath & Yahanpath, 2012). However, the barriers can be removed by providing more interactive online classes, better engagement with students, and strengthening collaborations that create new and better learning experiences.

The challenge, then, becomes addressing the needs of both lecturers and students within the context of a tertiary education sector that is becoming ever more pressured, and resource constrained. The marketing discipline may have some strategies to offer. According to The American Marketing Association, "Marketing is the activity, set of institutions, and processes for creating, communicating, delivering, and exchanging offerings that have value for customers, clients, partners, and society at large." (Kotler & Keller 2015). This chapter explores new concepts for delivering engaging, collaborative online learning experiences in tertiary education from a marketing perspective.

TRANSITION FROM F2F TO ONLINE LEARNING

Before the COVID–19 pandemic, F2F learning was the preferred mode of delivery from the perspective of Australian universities. Many lecturers were totally dependent on PowerPoint (PPT) slides to support their oral presentations in lectures. Also, because of their long histories and the difficulties facing new entrants, universities were able to charge premium prices for their services. However, border closures in early 2020 resulted in a significant decline in both local and international student intakes and the consequent decline in revenues has placed tremendous pressure on university finances. As a result, to compete and stay relevant, universities need to change their business model.

According to Kotler & Keller (2015), undifferentiated, differentiated, concentrated, and micromarketing strategies should all be considered. An undifferentiated marketing strategy, or mass marketing, entails creating a single message for an entire audience. Its counterpart in higher education is F2F learning, where most lecturers are wholly dependent on PPT slides to support their oral presentations. It is a one-size-fits-all approach and has long been the preferred strategy for most lecturers. A differentiated marketing strategy involves creating different messages for two or more market segments or target groups. Its educational equivalent would be the use of combinations of online quizzes, PPT slides, and recorded lectures to deliver material to students. Concentrated strategies are blended modes using online delivery features such as quizzes, case studies, and presentations. Blogging and chat box are examples of micromarketing strategies, where lecturers tailor-make online delivery to meet the different needs of individual students. All these strategies can be used by lecturers to increase student engagement. Differentiating their services from those of other education providers will be the main challenge facing higher education institutions in the coming decade.

Moving from undifferentiated to differentiated strategies by focusing on individual student needs using various online tools is the game changer. Online learning has been the norm of education providers for the past 18 months and will remain the preferred mode in the future. Not only is it cost effective, it also meets the individual needs of students, especially when the online platforms have a wide range of features for engaging students such as blogging, web mailing, and chatting. It also provides students with the opportunity and leisure to study from any location.

Marketing and sales skills emphasise the importance of customer retention and relationship building. Stronger relationships with customers lead to better outcomes for both sellers and customers.

Relationship-based sales is cost effective. The same applies to education. Communication and collaboration between the lecturer and student using online platforms helps to deliver messages quicker, promotes better understanding of the needs of students - especially if the students are from overseas – and fosters student engagement. The marketing cost for recruiting and retaining students is high. With international student enrolments currently declining, building relationships in a collaborative way can enable universities to attract and retain more students.

With better online learning platforms and tools, lecturers can more easily engage with students and assess their needs, enabling them to respond quickly to student queries. Some overseas students are reluctant to ask questions in a traditional F2F learning environment due to shyness. Online platforms can break down that barrier and from my experience help students become more highly engaged. Lecturers using online platforms have the tools needed to facilitate engagement better and challenge students' thinking and learning ability in a more friendly way. Rather than getting offended, students become motivated and then take the initiative in classroom discussions.

THE 3 CS OF ONLINE LEARNING: COMMUNICATION, COLLABORATION, AND COMMITMENT

According to Chickering and Gamson (1987), frequent contact between students and faculty during and after lectures is the most important method of motivating and engaging students, particularly during tough times. Connecting and communicating with students enhances their intellectual abilities and encourages them to think about their own values and future study options. It is vital for student motivation and engagement, especially during the transition from F2F to online learning. The lecturer's empathy and communications with students can reduce students' stress and anxiety and help them achieve their required learning outcomes.

In marketing, as we move from traditional to digital communication, changes in consumer behaviour are increasing the importance of communicating with customers. Businesses are using online platforms such as social media, email, and blogs to collaborate with customers. Similarly, collaboration is vital in tertiary education to enhance the student learning experience (Fox 2021). It requires knowledge about how collaborative learning can be effectively applied using online platforms and how technology can be optimally utilised to support online learning. The benefits of both are greater collaboration between customers (students) and universities (lecturers) and enhancement of student learning experiences and competencies. It also increases student cooperation, builds commitment towards learning, and strengthens academic integrity.

Fox (2021) suggested that some of the benefits of online learning in tertiary education are:

- Increased student engagement in the classroom
- Greater ability to create active learning spaces among students
- Enhanced student achievement in their academic program
- Development of necessary skills for future employability
- More self–individual experiences
- Better social–emotional learning skills; and
- Greater ability to work in a group environment that increases analytical thinking skills, critical thinking skills, and interactions.

ENGAGING STUDENTS WITH DIFFERENT LEARNING STYLES

Identifying and understanding the different learning styles of students is a challenging task. It is equivalent to understanding customer needs and wants by gathering relevant buyer information through research. According to Bateman & Snell (2012), the VARK model identifies four types of learner: (1) Visual learners who prefer acquiring information through illustrations such as examples and cues; (2) Auditory learners who would rather listen and are adept at converting spoken instructions into actions; (3) Reading learners who prefer to receive information in the form of text; and (4) Kinetic learners – the learners by doing - who like to figure out answers to questions and solutions to problems themselves using physical feedback cues.

To design appropriate online materials, lecturers first need to understand the learners' level of thinking. Bloom's Taxonomy (1956) identifies six levels of learning, from the three lower levels of remembering, understanding, and applying to the three higher levels of analysing, evaluating, and creating.

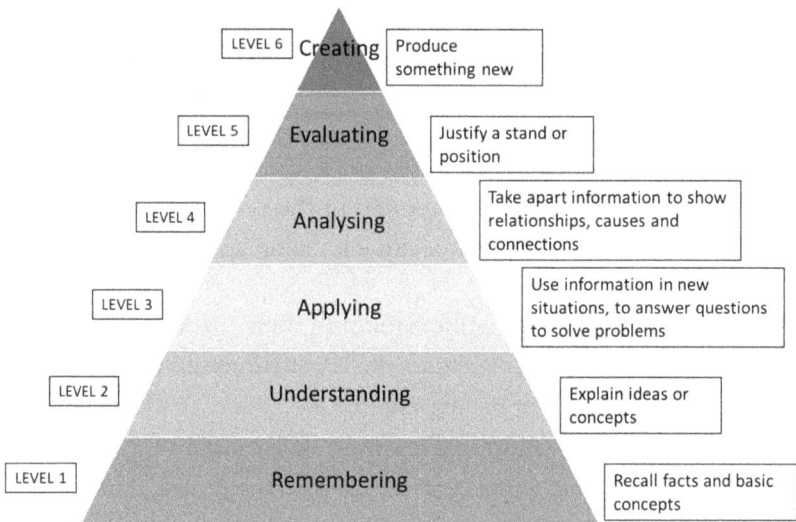

Figure 10 - Bloom Taxonomy (1956)

Level 1 is the most basic learning activity and entails remembering and recalling facts. Level 6 is the highest activity, involving creating something new. Lecturers need to determine students' thinking levels before designing online delivery resources such as PPT slides, blogs, case studies, and quizzes. They can do this by communicating with and getting feedback from students. Online platforms have the tools needed to implement this process.

When designing class activities, lecturers should frame tasks in ways that encourage students to defend their positions, reframe their ideas, listen to others' points of view, and articulate their points so they gain a complete understanding both as a group and as individuals. Students tend to be more engaged and learn more effectively when they are exposed to diverse viewpoints, especially those of people from different backgrounds. Lecturers should set tasks that allow students to think about the challenges they may encounter in their lives and help students to build new skills and capabilities. These skills may include:

- Listening to criticism and feedback
- Public speaking and active listening skills
- Critical thinking skills; and
- Cooperating with others.

ECONOMICS OF ENGAGING AND COLLABORATIVE LEARNING EXPERIENCES

The COVID–19 pandemic has led to changes in the business models of universities and other higher education providers, including a transition from the traditional F2F mode to a highly simulated online delivery method. Many universities have been downsizing staff and consolidating campuses in a more centralised location where lecturers can deliver online classes to larger numbers of students.

As noted by Kotler (2020), pricing is the only element in the marketing mix that earns revenue. International students, a major source of revenue, face significant difficulties, including studying in an unfamiliar environment, juggling study and work commitments, and commuting between campus, work, and home. Their choice to study abroad carries risks as well as benefits (Jude & Ryan, 2005).

Transitioning to the new business model using online platforms provides enormous benefits to universities and other higher education providers by enabling them to provide more effective learning, increase student numbers, and restore their revenue streams. It also benefits international students by allowing them to study from any location and providing them with access to tools that enhance collaboration, engagement, and learning.

Collaborative and engaging learning helps equip students with the skills and competencies they need for future jobs, including:

- Analytical skills and innovative mindsets
- Active learning skills
- Leadership and social skills
- Knowing how to use technology to enhance skills development
- Communication skills; and
- Complex critical thinking skills (Whiting 2020).

CONCLUSIONS

The future of F2F learning is bleak. From being the sole method of delivery for centuries, it has moved to a partnership role with distance learning and now online learning and may soon be largely replaced by online learning.

The tertiary education sector will continue to face challenges from decreasing international students, rising costs, and increasing competition. University managers and lecturers will need to constantly monitor and update online delivery methods as the needs and wants of students continue to change.

Universities should continue to enhance the relevance and quality of the education they provide students, especially those parts aimed at strengthening employability skills. They can do this by blending online and F2F delivery and by applying key marketing concepts to the ways in which the organise and deliver education.

REFERENCES

Bateman, T. and Snell, S. (2012). *Management: Leading and Collaborating in the Competitive World*, 10th ed., Australia: McGraw-Hill.

Bloom, B. (1956). *Taxonomy of Educational Objectives: The Classification of Educational Goals*, *https://www.google.com/search* accessed on 26/10/21

Chickering, A. and Gamson, Z. (1987). *Seven Principles for Good Practice in Undergraduate Education. https://eric.ed.gov/?id=ed282491*, accessed on 21/10/21

Carol, J. and Rayan, J. (2005). *Teaching International Students.* Oxon: Routledge

Fox-Jensen, E. (2021). *Collaborative Learning Methods, Tools, Research and Practical Models within a Digital Learning Environment*: Ethics, Caring and Sharing Design,' doi: 10.13140/8622.25308.10881/1.

Kotler, P., & Keller, K. (2016). *Marketing Management*, 15th edn, Pearson Education, England.

Shantha P. and Shan Y. (2012). *Power of Teaching by Walking Around. https://www.ft.lk/Opinion-and-Issues/power-of-teaching-by-walking-around/14-112876*, accessed on 21/10/21.

Whiting, K. (2020). *These are the top 10 skills of tomorrow*, World Economic Forum.

Chapter

11

The Impact of the Digital Workplace on Business Communication

Sue Cameron, Universal Business School Sydney

ABSTRACT

The digital workplace is the main driver of the recent changes in business communication. It has also significantly altered the content and delivery methods of teaching and learning. Interactions with students now require a new set of cognitive and physical skills. This chapter analyses the types of technical tools, applications, and elements of business communication within the digital workplace and their effects on the scholarship of students, lecturers, and educational institutions.

INTRODUCTION

The 21st Century and in particular the last decade has experienced significant changes in business communications mainly due to developments in information technology (infotech) and biological technology (biotech). The COVID-19 pandemic has increased the rate of change of these technologies to the extent that business communication is now almost totally digital.

The digital workplace has not only changed the way we work, but also the speed at what we are expected to work. This chapter discusses the impact on the workplace generally and on business communications specifically of Artificial Intelligence (AI) Deep Learning, 3D printers, and other contemporary and prospective platforms. It also addresses the current job market and makes some cautious predictions on how the market will change over the coming decades.

The influence of the digital workplace on both students and teachers has also been huge. A whole set of new skills, attitudes, and knowledge are now required for success. With technologies continuing to change rapidly, lifelong learning has become essential for everyone.

THE DIGITAL WORKPLACE IMPACT ON BUSINESS COMMUNICATION

Information technology is now the most important communication tool for organisations, with the Internet making business literally a virtual reality experience. Each advancement in technology – from the Farming revolution and the Industrial revolution to today's Digital revolution – seems to eclipse its predecessor in sophistication, complexity, and speed.

So, what is the digital workplace? Based on current research there appears to be several definitions ranging from the simple introduction of some technology to an integrated technology framework on a cloud-based platform that allows business to work in a virtual environment. The latter definition includes platforms that contain "all the applications, data, tools and collaboration features employees need to perform work within a secure online interface that they can access from anywhere, anytime and on any device". It streamlines/simplifies a complex range of technology tools.

Business communication has changed significantly over the past decade in three main ways:

- **Social Media** has forced people to develop a wider range of communication skills.
- **Virtual Offices** and the Internet have enabled people to work anywhere at any time and to communicate with their teams using platforms such as Zoom, Google Hangout, Skype, MS teams, and Blackboard Collaborate.
- **The Labour Force** has become more flexible, in line with the rapidly changing nature of work, which now comes in many forms - i.e., type, time, place, and pace. There is much more part-time and casual employment (the Gig economy) than in the past - e.g., 'Today around one in three employed people work part time, compared with one in ten 50 years ago' (RBA 2017).

TECHNOLOGIES THAT IMPACT ON BUSINESS COMMUNICATION

Artificial Intelligence (AI)

AI-based software is becoming more efficient and effective and is taking on more and more complex business communication tasks. Business communication must keep abreast of the changes and capabilities of this technology.

Cloud technology

This technology allows users to store and access data via the Internet rather than on a personal hard drive. The cloud offers huge benefits such as scalability, continuity, and security, The increase in storage capacity allows greater provision of Internet-based data and improved voice communication. It permits organisations to serve multiple and fluctuating communication needs.

Fifth generation mobile network technology (5G)

This is the next leap forward in mobile network technology. The main benefit is speed; downloads that used to take several minutes now require only a few seconds. Soon, mobile devices will be interconnected, and immersive experiences will be the norm. This means faster, more reliable, and more interesting business communication.

Deep Learning

This is a subset of machine learning, where artificial neural networks and algorithms inspired by the human brain learn from large amounts of data. It mimics how humans learn - from experience, processed by neural networks. The algorithms require a task to be performed repeatedly, each time tweaking it a little to improve the outcome. It is referred to it as 'deep learning' because the neural networks have various (deep) layers. Just about any problem that requires "thought" can be addressed by deep learning.

3D Printing (3D)

This is an additive manufacturing process that allows a physical object to be created from a digital design and raw materials such as powders, carbon fibres, and graphene. For students planning to enter the manufacturing sector a knowledge of 3D printing will be essential when future 3D printers handle mass production as quickly as and at lower cost than current mass-production methods. Although not currently relevant to business communication, who knows what the future use of this technology could be?

IMPACT ON STUDENTS AND TEACHERS

Teachers must be aware of the continuing trend toward a predominantly digital workplace when planning and delivering lessons to students. Structural changes in the labour force will affect the future of the students as there will be many more service jobs and fewer product jobs. For example, in manufacturing, 3D printers and robots are taking over ever more of the tasks that traditionally have been the preserve of manual workers.

However, these technical tools still need to be supervised and managed. Generally, students want and need management and leadership skills and more managers and leaders will be required in the future. An example of poor management is the Robodebt fiasco in Australia. (Robodebt was a method of automated debt assessment and recovery that was introduced in 2016 by Services Australia as part of its Centrelink payment compliance program. It replaced a slow but reliable manual system of calculating overpayments and issuing debt notices to welfare recipients.) A knowledge of these workplace changes will impact on the students' futures and therefore reshape the teaching of business communication.

The actual tasks involved in the digital workplace are less routine, due to the technological changes that have led to the more repetitive tasks being automated. Skills gaps continue to be high as the demand for skills across jobs changes. Employers are most concerned at the lack of professional business communication skills, especially the rising use of technical slang and abbreviations in text messages.

The interaction with students now requires a new set of cognitive and physical skills such as critical thinking, analytical thinking, problem solving, and skills in self-management such as active learning, resilience, stress tolerance, and flexibility. These skills may need to be taught as specific subjects due to their importance especially if cohorts are heavily weighted toward international students.

5G offers bandwidth to support ultra-high-definition video, allowing video conferencing to be more appealing and effective for remote work and study. According to several pieces of research employees/students are 75% more likely to watch a video than read text.

Information workers, employees, and students prefer newer communication tools, particularly instant messaging, over more traditional ones like e-mail or team workspaces (Deloitte 2021).

According to Accenture's latest Technology Vision research, 70% of global consumers expect their relationship with technology to be more prominent in their lives over the next three years. Visual communications will increase. As one of the three media forms of communication visual is now more important than ever. Why? Because students/people comprehend and retain visuals better than they do text.

THE TEACHING AND DELIVERY OF BUSINESS COMMUNICATION

Learning is no longer an internal, individualistic activity. Rather, it is a collaborative and social experience. It now links the formal learning agenda of educational institutions with the personal learning goals of students and with learning communities beyond the classroom. For example, Wikis, blogs, and podcasts are being used as a collective intelligence knowledge base for communication.

Online teaching requires more than just replicating the content, format, and delivery method of face-to-face teaching. Standing in front of a camera and broadcasting the same material in the same way as in a face-to-face class is not effective when teaching online, particularly when student engagement is important.

As discussed by Ashok Chanda (2021) in his interesting article, *The Art of Digitalising Online Content*, digital content must create a dynamic learning platform with material that engages students. Chanda believes that online learning is here to stay. Greg Whateley (2021), in his comprehensive paper, *Alternative Delivery Options*, states that the future lies in hybrid learning, which offers students the choice of face-to-face or online learning. The latter is of particular benefit for international students studying offshore, especially during unexpected crises like pandemics.

Research was conducted by UBSS to ascertain if its students prefer being online or on campus with face-to-face learning. The following graph indicates that during the last trimester of 2020 and Trimesters 1 & 2 of 2021 the majority preferred online learning. The main benefits cited by students were lower cost of travel and saving of time.

% of Students Who Preferred to Study Online

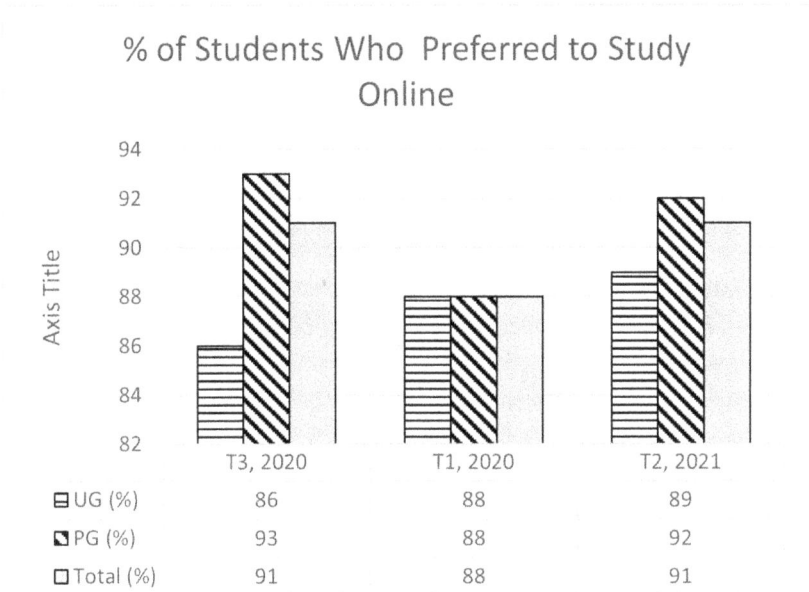

	T3, 2020	T1, 2020	T2, 2021
UG (%)	86	88	89
PG (%)	93	88	92
Total (%)	91	88	91

Figure 11 - % of Students Who Preferred to Study Online
(Source: UBSS Research)

The graph above shows a steady increase in undergraduate preference to study online, while postgraduate preference dipped in T1, but is back at 92% in T2. It will be interesting to study these trends in 2022 and 2023 or whenever the COVID 19 pandemic subsides or is controlled more effectively. At that stage will students miss the face-to-face interaction with their peers and lecturers and decide to return to campus?

In the Trimester 2 survey, students were asked to provide reasons for their expressed preference. As can be seen from the Word Cloud, the COVID virus is on the students' minds, with home and safety being paramount. Another factor in their decision is the time saving.

Teaching methods that have proven successful in the new digital environment include:

- Dividing the verbal lecture content into smaller chunks of information. As in TED talks, there should be no more than 20 minutes per chunk (verbal in this context means the use of words both written and oral).

- Including activities such as case studies, quizzes, fun competitions, leader boards, and gamification to assist with knowledge retention and problem-solving.
- When students are showing a willingness to participate, actively engaging them in the conversation—posing questions, inviting them to elaborate, and taking notes.
- Having short, interactive assessments to hold students' attention.
- Using visuals such as diagrams, pictures, and photos, as people are approximately 30% more likely to retain visuals than text; and
- Using videos. The widening coverage of 5G is increasing bandwidth availability and thus supporting ultra-high-definition video. It is making videos more appealing and effective for remote study.
- Having students use their webcams during class and assessments not only to comply with CPA's requirements of identification and observation, but also so the lecturer is cognisant that they are in attendance and can participate, thereby increasing engagement.

New and emerging pedagogical trends include:

- The move to opening-up learning and making it more accessible and flexible.
- The rise in sharing of power between lecturers and students.
- The increasing use of technology, not just in teaching but also in assisting and supporting students and providing new forms of assessment.

CONCLUSIONS

Our love of technology has allowed businesses to weave technology (and the businesses themselves) into the fabric of our lives. While this has transformed how we work, live, and interact with the world, it is important to recognise that this love for technology is not unconditional. It is becoming increasingly clear that communications and media businesses cannot assume that the customer is always looking for the latest tech or the best-of-the-best upgrade. They also want a sense of comfort and confidence that everything will just work as expected. (Accenture 2021)

Finally, in education today change is the only constant.

REFERENCES

Accenture (2021) *Communications and media technology Vision 2020* Retrieved from *https://www.accenture.com/us-en/insights/communications-media/technology-vision*

Chanda, A. (2021) *The efficacy of online studies.* Retrieved from *https://www.ubss.edu.au/media/2695/the-efficacy-of-online-studies*

Marshall, S. (2020) *The digital workplace defined* CMS WiRE, Retrieved from *https://www.cmswire.com/cms/social-business/what-a-digital-workplace-is-and-what-it-isnt-027421*

Reserve Bank of Australia (2017) *The rising share of part-time employment.* Retrieved from *https://www.rba.gov.au/publications/bulletin/2017/sep/3*

Whateley G. (2021) *Alternative Delivery Options.* Retrieved from *https://www.ubss.edu.au/articles/2021/september/alternative-delivery-options/*

Chapter

12

Cloud Accounting and Graduate Employability Skills

Mohammad Akbar, Universal Business School Sydney

ABSTRACT

Surveys conducted in three major Latin American (LATAM) countries in early 2020 showed that COVID-19 has created considerable uncertainty for students. However, they also showed that the sector has the capacity to make positive, permanent changes, and that institutions that are flexible and able to adapt quickly are most likely to succeed in the new and changed environment. The author discusses how institutional flexibility at UBSS allowed him to introduce a new digital tool in an accounting subject, and the effect this change had on student satisfaction and acquisition of key employability skills.

INTRODUCTION

The COVID-19 pandemic has caused severe problems for most higher education providers and their students. Providers have had to move abruptly from mainly face-to-face (F2F) to wholly online or distance-learning delivery, and students have had to accept the change in delivery mode while adjusting to lower and more uncertain incomes. However, the pandemic has also provided both providers and students with a much greater understanding and appreciation of online learning, including the importance of using highly functional and student-friendly online platforms and tools.

THE EY-PARTHENON SURVEYS

Prior to COVID-19, the share of students enrolled in online programs was only 15% in Mexico, 14% in Peru, and 8% in Colombia. The onset of COVID-19 and the ensuing quarantine forced the closure of all campuses in these countries, but with the requirement that the continuity of education be maintained. By the end of April 2020, higher education providers had agreed to move all delivery online. In the same month, teams from EY-Parthenon, a global strategy consulting organisation, conducted digital surveys of 4,800 higher-education students in these three countries. Their aim was to get a better understanding of both the short-term effects and the longer-term implications of the COVID-19 pandemic for the higher education sector in Latin America.

The surveys indicated that the short-term outcomes were mixed. Some providers, mainly in the private sector, were reasonably well-prepared for online delivery, but others, especially in the public sector, were not. The situation was the same for students, with some students being well-equipped to undertake online learning but many others not having access to broadband or to a computer or tablet in their homes. The situation was aggravated by a deterioration in personal economic circumstances. The EY-Parthenon teams found that 91% of Mexicans thought that the pandemic would have a negative impact on their salaries, with 64% already experiencing a decrease in income of at least 60% (Lytle, 2020). These developments had increased the demand for financial aid and tuition adjustments and had led many students to switch to free online education platforms like Udemy, Coursera, Skillsshare, EdX, and MasterClass.

The medium- and longer-term outlooks were also mixed. The surveys suggested that the less favourable economic conditions would reduce the demand for tertiary education. Students would also place greater importance on the functionality and user friendliness of EdTech platforms and tools. However, the prospect of an extended lockdown period would also be seen by some providers as an opportunity to expand their online capabilities. EY-Parthenon suggested that the providers that are the most flexible and can adapt most quickly would be best placed to exploit the opportunities for growth in the new online environment.

ESSENTIAL REQUIREMENT OF IMPROVING EMPLOYABILITY SKILLS

Business schools have structured units that students must pass to complete an accounting degree. Most accounting degrees require students to take two basic accounting units; two intermediate accounting units; a tax, a cost accounting, and an auditing unit; and perhaps an accounting information systems unit along with management, marketing, and other accounting specialisation units. To promote active learning, a strong connection between industry practitioners and academics is required. Increased emphasis is also being placed on experiential learning as educators focus on the new technological tools becoming available in the accounting industry. The challenge is for providers to meet, within a few classroom hours, all the requirements of the education provider while still preparing students for the CPA Exam. In many cases, it is left to employers to teach graduates the new technology skills they need to succeed in the accounting profession (PICPA, Articles, 2019).

There is a growing concern about the quality of higher education as graduates require job-ready training and participation in Continuing Professional Development (CPD) programs to meet industry requirements. When planning CPD for accountants at UBSS, it was found that in most cases there is a need for some hands-on training in the use of new technological tools.

According to Professionals Australia, CPD involves maintaining, enhancing, and extending knowledge expertise and competence of professionals, including:

- keeping up to date with technical developments in relevant area(s) of specialisation;
- extending knowledge into other relevant fields;
- honing existing skills and developing new ones;
- developing an understanding of the practical application of new skills and knowledge;
- applying learning and accumulating experience (Fitzell, 1970).

CHANGES TO AN ACCOUNTING SUBJECT AT UBSS

The author teaches IT for Accounting (BAC11) at UBSS. It is one of the units aimed at helping students develop their IT skills. Prior to Term 2, 2019, UBSS had used a stand-alone version of MYOB AccountRight to train students. However, well before COVID19, the UBSS lecturers recognised the need to move to online accounting software, since:

- students could only access MYOB when they were physically present in the UBSS computer lab, severely restricting their practice time; and
- students using MacBook faced great difficulty installing the free version of MYOB, making it hard for them to submit assignments on time.

After considerable research, UBSS decided to switch from MYOB to Xero. By the end of the term, it was clear that this was a good decision. Student participation improved. The accounting academics did not know about COVID-19 back then, but this change allowed them to avoid some major problems when the School was required, in early 2020, to switch to online delivery.

Xero has developed a special platform that allows educators to train learners with the same version that is used by professional accountants. The platform provides teachers with Administrator Rights, allowing them to monitor the progress of students. Also, due to a two-step authentication process, it is difficult for students to give access to any third party to do their assignments. Xero's online tools have made teaching and assessment more effective and much easier.

Without the demonstrations included on Xero, it is difficult to show students how accountants work in real life. UBSS lecturers can now demonstrate to students exactly how accountants process accounts receivable, accounts payable, payroll, and other transactions undertaken by a typical accounting department in an organisation.

At UBSS, students are learning with what is probably the most popular cloud-accounting software. As a result, they will be more employable when they graduate. The author has adopted this same model in other institutions at which he teaches, and at all places he has experienced more and better student participation. It is likely that the reason behind the improvement in learning is the realisation by students that accounting is not a boring, number crunching, and difficult job. By learning through Xero, they realise that accounting can be fun and easy, and as a result they involve themselves more actively in the learning process.

CONCLUSION

As with many other industries, digitisation is changing the way accountants work. Increased computing power and more sophisticated software are transferring most of the dull and repetitive tasks to computers, allowing humans to focus on more interesting activities that utilise their creativity and problem-solving skills. It is important that academics who are teaching accounting be fully aware of these changes so they can better prepare their students to work productively and efficiently as soon as they move from the university into the accounting profession.

REFERENCES

Fitzell, D. J. (1970, Jan 1). *The importance of continuing professional development.* Retrieved from: *http://www.professionalsaustralia.org.au/australian-government/blog/the-importance-of-continuing-professional-development/*

Lytle, R. (2020). *How COVID-19 has impacted higher education in Mexico, Colombia and Peru.* EY-Parthenon Education sector.

PICPA, Articles. (2019, Apr 19). Retrieved from PICPA - Pennsylvania Institute of CPAs: *https://www.picpa.org/articles/picpa-news/2019/04/23/pa-cpa-journal-prepping-accounting-students-for-a-new-tech-world*

Section 3:

Academic Management

Chapter

13

Alternative Delivery Options

Greg Whateley, Universal Business School Sydney

ABSTRACT

Because of the COVID-19 pandemic, there has been an involuntary shift to online learning – in its many manifestations. In turn, this has highlighted and facilitated a range of alternative modes of delivery for international students. These are sometimes referred to as flexible modes of delivery and at other times as alternative modes of delivery. The traditional face-to-face mode has been overtaken (certainly for a period) by a range of alternative arrangements that cater for lockdowns and community restrictions. Arguably, the most challenging part of these restrictions has been their unpredictability, making planning and strategy difficult. The option of having alternatives to face-to-face delivery ready and available is a most-valued commodity at present.

INTRODUCTION

Prior to the pandemic, international education (onshore in Australia) was in face-to-face mode, with strict regulations around: the percentage of classes allowed to be completed online by international students; attendance at face-to-face classes; the extent of employment hours permitted on a student visa; and progression rates (mostly 5 percent) needed to maintain a student visa. Much of this was dictated by the Australian ESOS Act 2000 and the supporting National Code. Then, of course, everything changed!

In truth, there has been a slow and determined movement in the regulations over a period of time. Matters such as attendance have been downplayed for a number of years for example. Working hours have been redefined (quite significantly in recent times) and even matters of progression have been either suspended or made more flexible to provide the support and compassion required when dealing with students under duress.

The so-called alternative (flexible) modes of delivery – Blended Learning (bLearning) as described by West (2021), Online Learning (eLearning) as outlined by Chanda (2021), Hybrid Learning (hLearning) as illuminated by Whateley (2021), and Mobile Learning (mLearning) were viewed previously as essentially domestic options with little if any application for international students studying in Australia. Certainly, those onshore. International students were provided with some of these options at the more progressive institutions – but usually under conditions and other restrictions. This, too, is no longer the case!

The rapid shift to online learning in 2020 created a precedent (some say a lightning rod) that is likely to stay with us for some time. The prediction is that even with a return to face-to-face learning in the years ahead the percentage of study permitted online for international students will grow to 50 percent of the load. This represents a significant shift in thinking and would be consistent with developments in other countries around the world.

Tertiary Institutions were required to move rapidly into eLearning – it was a matter of survival during the pandemic. Some of the better-prepared organisations (and many had been dabbling in alternative/flexible options for some time) managed to deviate even further and utilise the other modes with varying degrees of success. Sector reports suggest that the more flexibly inclined have fared best during the so-called international student crisis. There are several reasons for this. When the Australian Government regulations softened on the number of paid hours that international students can work in country, for example – from 40 hours per fortnight to unlimited – the demand, of course, for flexibility increased significantly. This will be a very difficult situation to reverse in the coming years. It is highly likely that flexibility will remain a constant feature as we move forward.

THE PERILS OF ENFORCED ELEARNING

The sudden switch to online (eLearning) caused a considerable amount of distress for many institutions and in particular for academic staff. For many staff this was the 'end of the world' as they knew it. Understandably, for those who had been teaching international students for many years in the traditional face-to-face mode this was indeed a precarious and uninvited demand – they were in fact 'digital convicts' (Whateley, 2020). For others it was the opportunity to put in place a variety of modes that could still maintain high levels of student engagement. Learner engagement (coupled with the student experience) – remember - is perceived as the end game.

The author's own institution appears to have fared well, with the most recent Student Feedback on Units (July 2021) scoring 4.4/5 (the highest score since record-keeping commenced in T1, 2016); Staff Satisfaction scoring 4.3/5; and 92 percent of students stating that they would prefer to stay online for the duration of their studies. Sector feedback suggests that the aggregate is lower than this.

Given the commitment made to technology upgrades and capital investment in lecture studios, these indicators are satisfying and to some degree a relief. Classrooms were quickly converted to lecture studios with roaming cameras, monitors, an upgraded learning management system, and a 'live' studio look and feel – all at considerable cost.

Staff training also became a priority. The notion of simply throwing staff online (and from remote locations) was not seen as either appropriate or viable. The key issue was a focus on learner engagement, and this could best be achieved with high quality delivery from a familiar environment. This again came with a cost – but the dividend has been worth it.

This approach is by no means the standard approach. Many institutions were thrown into chaos from the outset, have struggled with home delivery, and have reaped significant disapproval from students throughout the country. The notion of recycling low-end presentations has also met with considerable criticism and disappointment across the sector.

THE PITFALLS ASSOCIATED WITH RETURNING TO FACE-TO-FACE CLASSES ON CAMPUS

The return-to-campus movement has taken quite a few hits with flash lockdowns across the country. Some of the enforced lockdowns (Victoria has had six to date) have varied in length from 10 days to four months. The key issue has been the unpredictability of closures (and durations), especially in some States with hair-trigger border closures accompanied by circuit-breaker lockdowns – both with very short fuses – and very little time to prepare. In this context, face-to-face options seem dim - in truth doomed for the short term at least.

The very notion of opening up to face-to-face operations and then having to do an about-turn several weeks later in response to restrictions makes the task at best stressful, and at worst unmanageable. The process also creates unnecessary uncertainty for students. This is less an issue with business students than it is for applied science students.

Several providers have recently formally announced that they will continue online learning for the rest of 2021, some even predicting throughout 2022. The news has not been well received in many quarters. What the decision has done though, is provide a degree of certainty and consistency – which is not a bad development in itself. It would appear that online learning and its associated variations are here for some time. Some predict that they will endure well into 2022, possibly 2023.

THE FUTURE OF HYBRID LEARNING

Hybrid Learning (hLearning) appears to be the future - or certainly the mode for the next couple of years. The model is based on delivering live sessions online with the option for students to attend face-to-face by choice. It is not unlike the concept of 'live-to-air' television. Drawing from the analogy of the hybrid car – the driver makes the decision on the mode, and this can change as required along the journey.

The enormous advantage of the hLearning mode is the quick (and relatively easy) response mechanism to future lockdowns and restrictions. The acceptance of the notion of high-end hygiene and COVID safety are also well accommodated in this mode. The worst-case scenario is that the option of sitting in a classroom during a live delivery is suspended for a given period – but teaching and learning continue online without interruption. It is important to remember that the author's own institution has gauged through student survey that currently only 8 per cent of students are even interested in physically returning to campus.

The mode also provides students with the all-important option of on-campus/off-campus delivery. This is well received by students. For staff it requires delivery on site throughout the trimester/semester. This is less well received by staff – but for many, it is regarded as a necessary evil. The issue of staff teaching onsite is all about ensuring a quality output complete with the necessary technology standard and IT support. This standard and consistency of delivery are difficult (if not impossible) to replicate in the home-studio environment.

The impact on multiple site/campus delivery is now up for debate. In the face-to-face environment international students at multiple locations would receive dedicated, campus-bound delivery. This has changed significantly with a more centralised online delivery plus additional campus support required (face-to-face) as needed. This provides an extra swing on the notion of hybrid learning.

STAFF AND STUDENT PERCEPTIONS

At the heart of the COVID-19 scenario is the impact that the changes have had on the international student experience. There is a mixed response to online learning – and this is not surprising. At the same time, there has been considerable acceptance of the mode not only in Australia but internationally (Klebs et al, 2021). This has been accompanied by an acknowledgement of the validity and currency of online learning (along with its variations).

There has been a considerable focus on student and staff response to online learning and teaching – and the outcomes vary from institution to institution. Mechanisms such as student feedback on unit surveys; staff satisfaction surveys; student satisfaction with online learning surveys; national QILT surveys relating to the overall student experience (the 2021 data collection commenced in July 2021 and will be published in early 2022); industry group surveys; and a plethora of research surveys (both private and public) are all useful tools for gathering intelligence on and around student/staff satisfaction.

The essential issue is gathering the data – and most importantly using the findings to improve delivery. Keeping abreast of state and national trends is important. The best source of meaningful feedback though is internal survey. It is essential that all providers have a clear understanding of their own student/staff needs and respond quickly and appropriately to the needs expressed. Acting on national feedback can be useful, but nothing beats listening carefully to your own cohorts and acting promptly and decisively. If supported appropriately, the outcomes and levels of satisfaction can be highly credible and satisfying for all stakeholders.

Using the ongoing data collected provides a genuine opportunity to enhance both the student experience and learner engagement. The author's School is an independent business school. It appears that onsite activities are currently not a high priority for students. Lecturer engagement and eResourcing, on the other hand, have become vital elements in the learning and teaching effort. This may not be the case with other institutions – but the important fact is that it is the key to this Institution's success.

CONCLUSION: WHAT DOES INTERNATIONAL STUDENT LEARNING AND TEACHING LOOK LIKE MOVING FORWARD?

Online learning will be with us for some time – well into 2023. With the likely opening of international borders in mid-2022 (still speculative) we will see a significant return of student numbers – some say a tsunami-like event. Others are more conservative, – but most agree that there will be a return in solid numbers.

The prediction, though, is not a return to the 'way things were' but rather to a more mixed-mode approach to learning and teaching. This mix will likely include up to 5 percent online, a partial return to face-to-face (as it was) and alternative options (blended, hybrid and mobile) changing the international education landscape for the better.

This may impact significantly on the notion of completing the full degree onshore. Students may opt for the online option offshore (for example) with only partial completion onshore. This will require a rethink in terms of visa regulations – but may in fact be a viable approach. A number of institutions – forced by the pandemic conditions – have significant numbers of students currently offshore studying online. To some degree this has changed the thinking around the issue.

REFERENCES

Australian Government, Department of Education, *Skills and Employment*. (2021) Retrieved from *https://internationaleducation.gov.au/regulatory-information/Education-Services-for-Overseas-Students-ESOS-Legislative-Framework/National-Code/Pages/default*

Chanda, A. (2021) *The efficacy of online studies.* Retrieved from *https://www.ubss.edu.au/media/2695/the-efficacy-of-online-studies*

Klebs, S. (et al) (2021) *One year later – COVID-19's impact on current and future college students.* Retrieved from *http://thirdway.imgix.net/pdfs/one-year-later-covid-19s-impact-on-current-and-future-college-students*

West, A. (2021). What is meant by blended learning? Retrieved from *https://www.ubss.edu.au/media/2716/what-is-meant-by-blended-learning*

Whateley, G. (2020) *Full marks for educators - the digital convicts of COVID-19.* Retrieved from *https://www.campusreview.com.au/2020/09/full-marks-for-educators-the-digital-convicts-of-covid-19/*

Whateley, G. (2021) *Understanding hybrid delivery.* Retrieved from *https://www.ubss.edu.au/media/2670/understanding-hybrid-delivery*

Chapter

14

OPM is not just another TLA

Andrew West, Universal Business School Sydney

ABSTRACT

As with many other industries, higher education is filled with Three Letter Acronyms (TLA), such as CRM, SMS, SIS, LMS and FTE. However, Online Program Management (OPM) is not just another TLA. Rather, OPM has the potential to revolutionise higher education design, management, analytics, content standardisation, distribution, and delivery. The theme of this round of the UBSS Publication Series includes updating and enhancing unit content and delivery. Many of the chapters address an individual field of study or subject. However, there is a revolution occurring in higher education that will totally change how unit content is developed, the way and by whom it is delivered, the student experience, and the business models that manage these. This chapter outlines current developments in OPM and presents four scenarios on how OPMs will change higher education during the 2020s.

INTRODUCTION

There is a revolution occurring in education right now. It is happening on our higher education campuses, in our homes and workplaces, and in cyberspace. It is the normalisation of online learning and its derivatives – hybrid learning and blended learning.

With the acceptance and growth of online, hybrid, and blended learning, higher education providers are looking for greater scale, capability, and flexibility in catering to rapidly changing education markets. OPM providers are helping universities achieve these goals by building, recruiting students for, and distributing their online programs. The global OPM market, which was valued at US$3.9bn in 2020, is projected to reach US$7.7bn in 2025 (HolonIQ, 2021). In the United States, there were over 60 global OPM providers at the end of 2020, and an additional 450 partnership agreements were signed in the first 6 months of 2021. All 40 Australian universities either have an OPM partner or are looking to establish a partnership by 2022.

IMPACT OF COVID-19 ON DELIVERY MODES

Professor Stephen Parker, former Vice Chancellor of the University of Canberra, observed that the traditional university "is closed and does everything itself. It's a closed and integrated organisation. And the idea of being a community runs deep. But there are many forces at work now, which make the model hard to maintain. It is inefficient to hold all of that capability in house when you're not using it all the time." (Hair, 2021)

COVID-19 has become the great accelerator of many social and technological trends. The normalisation of online delivery and its increasing acceptance by higher-education students is one of those trends. It is challenging universities to move away from their traditional, closed model. Following the onset of the COVID-19 pandemic, universities were forced to move all subjects online within weeks. They achieved this through bespoke applications at a subject-by-subject level. The result is a highly varied learning experience for students based on the ability of each lecturer to transform their traditional learning material into online format and deliver it to students using diverse channels of communication.

COVID-19 has accelerated the emergence of a new normal, involving students learning both remotely and face-to-face. Increasingly, students accept online learning, either stand-alone or as part of a blended offering. At UBSS, student feedback surveys (SFUs) conducted over the last four semesters have returned a 90% or higher preference for online learning. Qualitative responses include short-term themes of COVID impact and safety, and longer-term themes of convenience, time and money saved from reduced travel, lower cost of living by relocating away from Sydney to the regions and caring for family.

Pre-COVID-19, the twin successes of Australian universities of (1) progressively moving up the world research rankings and (2) becoming the No. 2 destination for international students, only behind the United States, were interlinked. To fund the research and expand their infrastructure, universities relied heavily on revenue from the international student market, which peaked in 2019 when 440, 667 international students provided fee revenue of AU$37.6 billion (27.3% of the total revenue of Australian universities) (APH, 2021).

With the subsequent decline in onshore international students and no substantial increase in funding from the Federal Government, the higher education sector faces the problem of delivering online modes efficiently and at scale while maintaining quality teaching and learning. Outsourcing to OPMs may be, at least in part, an effective solution.

GENESIS OF OPMS

OPMs are a 21st century phenomenon. Academic Partnerships was founded in 2007 and was quickly followed by 2U (whose partners include Harvard and Johns Hopkins Universities) in 2008. The total number of OPMs increased to more than 60 in 2020.

Gartner (2021) defines OPMs as providers that "offer a suite of services either as a package or on a fee-for-service basis. These services include market research, student recruitment and enrolment, course design and technology platforms, student retention, and placement of students in employment or training opportunities." (Gartner, 2021).

OPMs provide services and support over the whole student life cycle, from initial inquiry all the way to internships and employment services. They are more than just Learning Management Systems (LMS) such as Moodle, Blackboard, and Canvas. They are also more than Massive Online Open Courses (MOOCs) such as Coursera and edX. OPMs aim to use the brand and reputation of the universities and provide a complete suite of services, including instructional design and even course content in the online environment.

Students at universities that use an OPM are generally not aware that they are studying via an outsourced third-party provider. They assume that the lecturers and tutors are the same as those teaching on-campus. Universities do not mention that private companies are helping them run their online degrees. The private third party usually takes 60% of the tuition fees. This is due to the large marketing budgets and fat profit margins of online delivery, where after the initial development costs are covered, the variable cost of delivery is very low, but subject tuition fees remain at the same level. 2U's 43% margin is split evenly between the university and the OPM. (Carey, 2019)

CONSOLIDATION AND GROWTH OF THE OPM MARKET

To provide the full suite of services, a series of Mergers and Acquisitions (M&A) has occurred in the Education Technology industry over the last year. This has seen OPMs acquiring LMS platforms and MOOCs, providing both parties with a wider range of services.

The size of the global OPM market stands at $3b+ with 60+ OPMs worldwide. An increasing acceptance of online learning sees more universities launching online degrees, with the OPM market expected to reach $7.7b by 2025. Both growth and M&A have accelerated during 2021. They include the 2U acquisition of edX, Keypath Education's initial public offering (IPO), Noodle acquiring Hotchalk, Zovio expanding its services to become an OPM, the merger of Anthology and Blackboard, and Moodle's acquisition of three companies (Hill, 2021). 2U's recent acquisitions indicate how a suite of offerings can be assembled under the one umbrella, with Get Smarter (Short Courses), Trilogy (Bootcamps) and EdX (MOOC) all purchased recently to enable higher education and workforce up-skilling to be provided together.

GROWTH OF OPMS

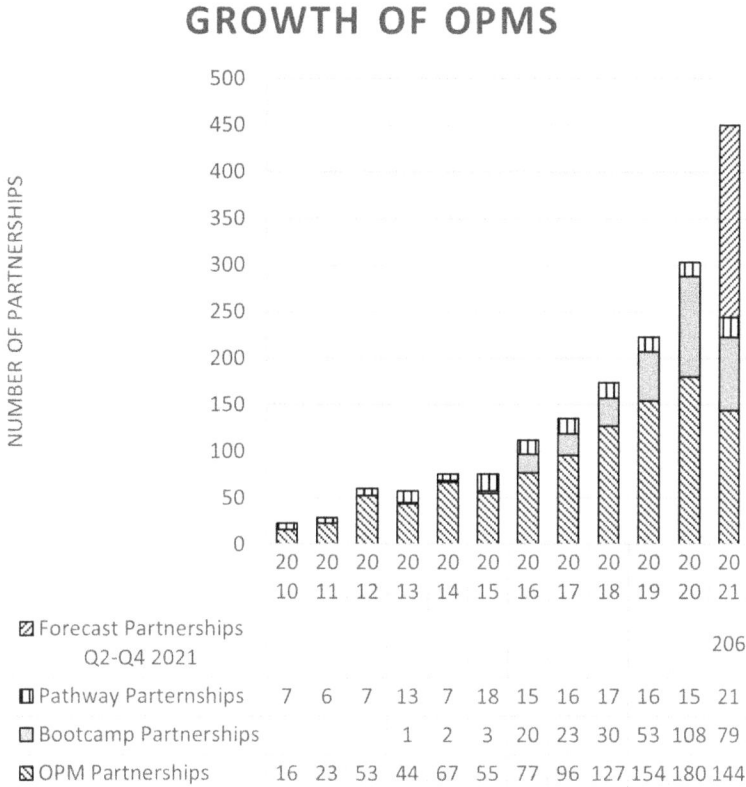

	2010	2011	2012	2013	2014	2015	2016	2017	2018	2019	2020	2021
Forecast Partnerships Q2-Q4 2021												206
Pathway Parternships	7	6	7	13	7	18	15	16	17	16	15	21
Bootcamp Partnerships				1	2	3	20	23	30	53	108	79
OPM Partnerships	16	23	53	44	67	55	77	96	127	154	180	144

Figure 12 - Number of new University Partnerships established with OPMs, Bootcamps and International Pathways, 2010-2021

It is estimated that the top 10 OPM's receive half of global OPM revenue (HoloIQ, 2021). The Herfindahl-Hirschman Index (a measure of market concentration) for the global OPM market contains 250 to 350 companies, which suggests that the market is competitive. It is one of the least concentrated of the global technology markets, indicating there is room for further mergers and acquisitions for consolidation at the top end of the market.

THE IMPACT OF OPMS ON CONTENT AND DELIVERY

The traditional model of the design, development, and delivery of university content assumes that all activities are conducted in-house. Within a particular faculty, courses are designed based on desired graduate attributes and course outcomes. They are developed by the internal university lecturer or unit co-ordinator, usually based on an external text from a world-renowned subject matter expert. "Universities must have clear course architectures underpinned by pan-university strategies for designing courses, developing content and delivering teaching and learning." (Orton, 2021). The traditional model is based on highly fragmented silos of knowledge within the university which rely on insourcing for the design and delivery of learning materials, as well as student services.

As noted earlier in this chapter, OPMs are external global organisations offering a full range of software solutions across the whole student experience. The students are often unaware that an external organisation has designed and delivered the learning material, assuming it was all provided by the university. The opportunity for cross-university delivery is particularly the case for professional and technically based degrees such as engineering, information technology, nursing, accounting, and teaching. Due to a state or nationally based professional body accrediting the qualification, this provides national standards of proficiency and expertise in a particular field to deliver the skills, knowledge and attributes required of that profession. This is especially so at the undergraduate level. The question this raises is - if there is a national standard and recommended course materials are provided by national professional bodies, why are these not developed, designed, and delivered at a national level across all higher education providers?

OPMs may be the answer to this question, with their ability to develop programs at scale and distribute these through the universities and other higher education providers, relying on the universities' brands for recognition, facilities, and the teacher-related and ancillary services expected from higher education providers. However, this is not a straight-forward development, with many economic, political, and social interests impacting the outcome. Who will design, develop, and deliver the learning material and who will keep the revenue generated from this process are questions that cannot yet be answered with any certainty.

The two main drivers of these scenarios are (1) the probability of further consolidation of the higher education services industry, from what is currently a quite fragmented base, and (2) the forces of outsourcing against the continued insourcing of specialised material. Set out below are four possible scenarios through to the end of this decade that have been proposed by the education technology consultancy HolonIQ (2021).

1. Consolidation/Outsource. This scenario sees the growth and consolidation of global players in the OPM market as providing a wider range of remotely delivered student services, online teaching, and other learning services. As in many of the other global technology markets, oligopolies with great market power form to dominate their markets. This is the natural result of the maturity of OPMs, with a consolidation of industry standards and professional bodies. A few OPMs with a complete range of service offerings dominate, with smaller niche providers forming from opportunities of social change and new technology. Universities have input into the content, but focus more on research and industry partnerships, while handing over the delivery of learning material to the OPMs. These OPMs will in turn become targets of the global giant technology companies, as they offer access to the billions of global students.

2. Fragmentation/Outsource. OPMs grow, but new players continue to enter the market. Universities maintain control of the design and development of learning material as well as student services. They do not commit to the complete suite of bundled options from the OPMs. This maintains the competition for OPMs with many providing fee-for-service and commoditised offerings. The success of this scenario is reliant on the universities resourcing and building the key capabilities of course content, which is likely, but less likely is online instructional design, cloud-based technologies, and student user experience required.

3. Consolidation/Insource. Universities co-ordinate their online offerings including student services in a pan-

university network. This would be a centralised public alternative to the private OPMs. The higher education providers create a networked approach, relying less on OPMs and more on their intra-university collaboration based on commonalities, such as regional or professional disciplines. Given the continuing competition between universities in Australia and their inability to move beyond their own silo offerings to attract students, this scenario has a low probability of being realised. Similar to scenario 2, it requires resourcing and capability development, as well as collaboration.

4. Insource/Fragmentation. Universities build their own in-house capabilities at the scale and quality of the private OPMs. The universities retain and reverse the current trend of qualified staff leaving to be employed in private OPMs, taking their knowledge and skill base with them. This scenario requires a strategic re-alignment by universities away from buildings and capital works to investments in online, cloud-based infrastructure and staff development to be able to compete with the global power of the OPMs. It is most likely to be realised among specialised and niche higher education providers with a small student cohort and a strong focus on research and development.

CONCLUSION

Whatever happens in Australia is small fry compared to movements in the United States. Just as the FAANGs of US technology impact on all industries, it is the OPMs from the States that have the resources, scale, and attractive business models for the existing high education sector. The Australian EdTech players are minnows compared to the great blue whales of the OPMs, which move relentlessly through the global oceans of the higher education sector. The recent impact of COVID-19 in accelerating the uptake of technology, the social change of normalisation of online learning, and the decrease in revenue for Australian universities through closed borders to international students have heightened the likelihood that the influence of global OPMs in Australian higher education will increase substantially in the coming decade.

REFERENCES

APH (2021). *Overseas students in Australian higher education: a quick guide* Updated 22 April 2021.
https://www.aph.gov.au/About_Parliament/Parliamentary_Departments/Parliamentary_Library/pubs/rp/rp2021/Quick_Guides/OverseasStudents, viewed 25th September, 2021.

Carey, K (2019). *The Creeping Capitalist Takeover of Higher Education.* Huffpost, *https://www.huffpost.com/highline/article/capitalist-takeover-college/*, viewed 20th September 2021.

Gartner (2021). *Online Program Management in Higher Education.* *https://www.gartner.com/reviews/market/online-program-management-in-higher-education*, viewed 26th September 2021.

Hare, J (2021). *Online Boom Ahead as Unis Outsource Teaching.* Australian Financial Review, 24 May 2021 edition.

Hill, P (2021). *OPM Market Landscape and Dynamics Summer 2021 Updates. https://philonedtech.com/opm-market-landscape-and-dynamics-summer-2021-updates/*, viewed 25 September 2021.

HolonIQ (2021). *244 University Partnerships in the First Half of 2021.* *https://www.holoniq.com/notes/opm-mooc-opx.-244-university-partnerships-in-the-first-half-of-2021/*, Viewed 24 September 2021.

Orton, T and Curry-Hyde, E (2021), *Our Universities Have Been Gold Medallists Before, Here's How they can do it again* – Nous Group. *https://www.nousgroup.com/insights/universities-gold-medallists/*, viewed 2nd October, 2021.

OPM is not just another TLA

Chapter

15

Lecturer Support and Student Feedback During the Pandemic

Anurag Kanwar, Universal Business School Sydney

ABSTRACT

The COVID-19 pandemic has forced the higher education sector in Australia to move from mainly face-to-face to wholly online delivery. In this Chapter, the author uses her own experience as a lecturer at three different institutions to highlight the variety of ways in which the sector has managed the transition, including the provision of support for lecturers and the use of student feedback on the effectiveness of teaching.

INTRODUCTION

The pandemic-induced change from face-to-face to online delivery has led, unsurprisingly, to a sharper focus on change management including the need to support lecturers as they adapt to a new and unfamiliar mode of delivery and to consider the change in learning environment when assessing student responses to teaching. In higher education an important vehicle for obtaining information about student responses is student feedback surveys. Students are invited to provide anonymous responses to a questionnaire about their learning experience. The questionnaire includes questions on unit content and assessments, student resources, and the lecturer's teaching performance. This chapter describes the author's experiences with institutional support of lecturers and the use of student feedback during the early days of the pandemic in New South Wales (NSW).

INSTITUTIONAL RESPONSES

In mid-March 2020, the NSW government ordered a complete or partial lockdown of all but the most essential businesses. Education was severely impacted. Students were only allowed to attend face-to-face classes if they could not learn from their homes. Since virtually all students in NSW have access to computers and the Internet, the lockdown effectively brought an end to face-to-face delivery. However, the approach and effort put into the transition to online learning differed markedly among institutions, including three at which the author was teaching.

Institution 1

This higher education provider, referred to as Institution 1, sent an email to all academic staff telling them to stay at home and, from the following Monday, commence teaching online. There was no support offered to help lecturers make the transition to online learning. Lecturers were simply informed that they were to access the Zoom platform and use their own personal devices to deliver their lectures and learning materials.

Institution 2

The second provider, denoted here as Institution 2, also took the initial step of sending an email to academic staff. However, this email advised staff that classes would be suspended for two whole weeks, to give both lecturers and students sufficient time to prepare properly for the move to online learning. Lecturers were advised that they would be required to deliver their lectures on-campus, where they would be provided with purpose-designed studios equipped with state-of-the-art facilities and cameras and supported with onsite IT specialists. Thus, students would be assured of high-quality delivery and staff would not be pressured to upgrade home-office equipment, which was in short supply following announcement of the lockdown.

Institution 3

The third provider, referred to as Institution 3, informed lecturers that at the beginning of the following week all classes would be moved online. Lecturers were directed to use Microsoft Teams and to upload their course materials to Google Drive. No additional support was offered.

STUDENT FEEDBACK SURVEYS

Institution 1

The classes at this institution were delivered on a free-of-charge Zoom platform, and in the first class delivered by the author Zoom cut out after 45 minutes. Fortunately, the author was able to direct students to an alternative platform and complete the session. Later, on their feedback forms, the students complained about the online learning platform, noting that it had not provided a pleasant experience for them or the lecturer. Many students complimented the lecturer for providing an alternative platform and for her innovative ideas such as establishing a YouTube channel and using Google Hangout. The lecturer received the highest ratings across all classes offered by the Institution in this teaching period.

Nevertheless, the lecturer's overall experience with the student feedback from this particular class was very disappointing – and quite bizarre. One student out of the 35 in the class used the feedback form to direct complaints against her. This student criticised the lecturer's hairstyle, her accent (which was deemed too Australian), and her behaviour towards this student (which the latter characterised as unprofessional). The Dean then asked the lecturer to attend a one-on-one session to discuss the complaints. The lecturer asked for a copy of the student's feedback form but was told that it could not be given to her because of 'privacy concerns.' Instead, the lecturer was told to come back for a later meeting.

The lecturer decided to push for a copy of the feedback form anyway and sought the support of senior management. She stated, correctly, that the allegations made in the feedback form had nothing to do with her teaching style or any other objective matter that related to effective learning. Rather, they reflected the student's subjective perception of the lecturer's appearance and behaviour. The lecturer asked how changing her hairstyle could improve the student's learning experience.

The senior academic leaders then questioned the lecturer about the accusation of 'unprofessional conduct' which, they advised, could be construed as bullying by the lecturer of a student from a culturally and linguistically different background. The lecturer pointed out that no other student had made such a complaint. She also reminded the Dean that one student in her class had approached for her for free legal advice about a matter affecting the student and a family member. The lecturer had notified the Dean of this request and had been told to ignore it. Fortunately, the lecturer had kept copies of the emails the student had sent asking for the legal advice. The emails had continued throughout the semester, even after the lecturer had referred the student to other sources of legal advice. It became apparent during the meeting with senior management that it was this student who had complained about the lecturer and that the complaint had nothing to do with the effectiveness of her teaching. Rather, it was about her refusal to provide the student with free legal advice.

It took three months to resolve this issue. By that time, the next teaching session was well under way and, not surprisingly, the lecturer had not been invited back to teach. This is not an unusual occurrence in the sector. The whole experience for the lecturer was extremely unpleasant, very confronting, and totally unfair.

Institution 2

As noted earlier, lecturers at this Institution were required to deliver their material from fully equipped lecture-studios located on campus. Each studio was equipped with tracking cameras, excellent audio, and live-chat facilities. Instead of Zoom, which is a general-purpose, video-conferencing platform, the institution used Blackboard Collaborate, which is a dedicated, virtual classroom tool. Teaching and learning materials were uploaded to the student platform in real time. All staff were provided with training on how best to teach in an online environment.

At the end of the trimester, Management informed lecturers that it was fully aware that that the teaching period had been extremely challenging for both staff and students and that this might be reflected in some aspects of the student feedback. Thus, any lecturer who received a poor result was invited to meet with their program director, discuss the feedback, and together derive learnings from it. The lecturers were very appreciative of this supportive approach.

In fact, the feedback from students at this institution was very positive. They reported that the online learning environment had strongly mirrored that of the traditional, face-to-face classroom environment. Further, about 90% indicated that they would prefer to stay online in later teaching periods. In this case, the lecturer was congratulated for her cooperation in continually coming to campus to teach the students and for the quality of her teaching. This has motivated her to put even more effort into improving the quality of her teaching materials and delivery.

Institution 3

While this institution required academic staff to teach using Microsoft Teams, it also told them not to use Microsoft Teams when recording their lectures. The reason given was that Microsoft Teams was not compatible with the Institution's learning management system.

Unfortunately, this led to an almost comical scenario where a lecturer would open the learning management system on one device and record the lecture using another device. The lecturer would then upload the recorded lecture to the Learning Management System Platform. All learning materials had to be uploaded to both the Learning Management System and the Cloud as some students were living overseas and could not access the Learning Management System. The time taken for such administrative activities was an additional 1-2 hours per week. The lecturers were not compensated for this additional demand on their time.

Predictably, at the end of semester the students complained about the ad hoc nature of the teaching. Most students in the author's class could not manage to work out the Teams System. The lecturer repeatedly asked the Institution for additional support for students (especially those who were overseas) but this was denied on every occasion. The feedback surveys indicated that students were extremely dissatisfied with their learning experience. The overseas students also expressed considerable anger that the timetable had not been adjusted to take into account the different time zones of the online students, and a large proportion had to be ready at 3am to access their class.

What was also surprising was that the author was asked to attend a meeting with management to explain the poor student results for her subject. The lecturer pointed out that the criticisms of the students were not in relation to her teaching style or the learning material. Rather, they were in relation to the poor technical support provided to the students by the Institution. This was not agreed to by the Institution's management, which claimed that the lecturer 'should have done more'. At this point the lecturer was informed that due to the negative student feedback she would be replaced.

CONCLUSIONS

Student feedback is a useful tool that can help managers of educational institutions evaluate the quality of the teaching provided to students. However, it is important that the feedback relates to teaching effectiveness. Some students use student feedback simply to criticise lecturer characteristics and behaviours that have no relationship with teaching effectiveness. Giving credence to these criticisms does not serve the interests of either the student or the lecturer.

REFERENCES

https://www.ubss.edu.au/articles/2021/may/online-teaching-a-tale-of-two-institutions/

https://www.smh.com.au/national/what-goes-wrong-when-uni-students-mark-their-teachers-20210831-p58nk0

https://www.smh.com.au/national/what-goes-wrong-when-uni-students-mark-their-teachers-20210831-p58nk0

https://www.ubss.edu.au/articles/2021/september/alternative-delivery-options/

https://www.ubss.edu.au/articles/2021/may/online-teaching-a-tale-of-two-institutions/

Chapter

16

The Contentious Role of Student Evaluations of Teachers

Angus Hooke, Universal Business School Sydney

Greg Whateley, Universal Business School Sydney

Anurag Kanwar, Universal Business School Sydney

ABSTRACT

The use of SETs for evaluating instructors and courses is a controversial, sometimes political, and often hotly debated issue in many college and university staffrooms. Some instructors and administrators argue that the information provided by SET ratings and comments helps them perform their roles more effectively, while others (mainly instructors) maintain that the instrument has biases and other weaknesses that make its use counterproductive. The effectiveness of the instrument also depends on the participation rate, which appears to be substantially lower for online learning. This chapter discusses the advantages and disadvantages of SETs and makes suggestions on how they can best be used in both face-to-face and online learning environments.

INTRODUCTION

Student Evaluations of Teaching (SETs) is an instrument used by education providers to collect and organise data on student ratings of instructors and courses. At UBSS, the tool is referred to as

Student Feedback on Units (SFUs). Typically, the ratings are collected toward the end of the teaching period (e.g., a trimester), often in the final revision class when most students are likely to be present. The data are obtained through structured surveys that may be paper based but increasingly are online (e.g., through Survey Monkey).

The surveys require students to rate characteristics of their instructor (such as how well prepared they are for class; feedback provided; use of technology; availability outside of class; and overall quality of teaching) and the course (e.g., its usefulness, achievement of learning outcomes; workload manageability; and clarity of assessment). The ratings are usually on a 7-point or 5-point Likert scale where, for the latter, 1 might indicate "Strongly disagree", 2 "Disagree", 3 "Neither agree nor disagree", 4 "Agree", and 5 "Strongly agree". Students are also encouraged to provide open-ended comments, where they give their opinions on the teaching and the course using free-form text.

UBSS has been collecting SET/SFUs in a systematic way since 2016 using a standard set of 11 questions.

Table 9 - Standard set of SET/SFU questions

	Survey Question
Q1	The subject provided useful knowledge and skills
Q2	The learning outcomes were achievable
Q3	The subject workload was manageable
Q4	The subject helped to develop relevant professional skills such as problem solving and critical thinking
Q5	The lecturer was well prepared for each class
Q6	The lecturer provided useful feedback
Q7	The lecturer had a good knowledge of the subject matter
Q8	The lecturer used e-learning resources e.g. smartboard Moodle in a way that aided learning in the subject
Q9	The lecturer was available to discuss learning problems outside of class time
Q10	The assessment requirements were clearly explained
Q11	Overall, the teaching in the subject was of high quality

The responses to the structured survey are used to compute means for each and all characteristics of each instructor and each course, as well as means for all instructors and all courses across programs and faculties. Some institutions also identify median values for the overall means of instructors as well as other measures designed to provide useful information for users.

Relevant SET/SFUs outputs (statistical measures and comments) are made available to instructors after exam results for the trimester have been processed. Each instructor receives a personalised file showing their mean scores for individual items as well as an overall score for their teaching and their course. They are normally provided with the faculty means – and sometimes the medians - for teaching and the course. A few institutions also give the percentile score for the instructor's teaching, probably the best indicator of their performance relative to those of their colleagues.

Selected SET ratings are also normally provided to administrators, who use them as an input into decisions about curricula and courses and about hiring, promotion, tenure, merit-increases, and training for instructors. Most higher education providers have a standard for SET ratings against which the results for individual instructors and courses are compared. A typical standard for a 5-Likert SET might specify that a rating in the range 4.6 – 5 is Outstanding, 4.3-4.5 is Very Good, 4.0-4.2 is Satisfactory, and Below 4 is Unsatisfactory. The bottom category might trigger corrective responses such as training support for the instructor, or modification of the content or design of the course.

HISTORY

Formal SET ratings have been collected for about a century. In the 1920s, Herman Remmers (Purdue University) and Edwin Guthrie (University of Washington) independently developed SET instruments with the intention of providing feedback to instructors on how students viewed their teaching (Stroebe, 2020). Administrators quickly saw the potential of SET ratings for increasing student engagement, improving courses and teaching, and evaluating the performance of instructors seeking employment, promotion, tenure, or pay rises. As a result, the proportion of US colleges using SETs increased to 29% in 1973, 68% in 1983, and 94% in 2010.

EVALUATION

SETs and students

Students undertake tertiary studies for a variety of reasons, including gaining the formal qualifications needed to enter a particular profession and the specific knowledge and skills needed to be successful in that profession. The SET process (collecting, organising, disseminating, and evaluating data on student ratings) provides them with a convenient and anonymous vehicle for expressing their approval or disapproval of part or all of the learning opportunities being provided to them and for making suggestions that might improve the offering in later trimesters.

Since their studies extend over several years, and those years can be among the most challenging in their lives, students also want their educational experience to be as convenient and enjoyable as possible. Many studies judge the validity of SETs by looking only at how well they measure student learning. However, student satisfaction is a legitimate goal and for many students may be an important mediating variable between institutional resources and student learning.

Not all students place value on the opportunity to provide feedback, as is indicated by the low natural participation rates and the efforts that education providers make to increase participation. This might be because students are generally satisfied with the offering, think their input will not have a significant impact, or don't have any interest in the future performance of the education provider. However, since the cost to students of participating in the data collection process is minimal and many students do value having a voice, it is likely that the net benefit to those who participate exceeds the net cost to those who see little or no personal value in the exercise.

Sets and instructors

Instructors want to be good teachers. For this, they need feedback on what is working and what needs to be improved. Students are well qualified to address most statements on a typical SET form since they have been exposed to the instructor's content, teaching aids, and methods of delivery for almost a whole trimester (traditionally about 12 weeks) by the time the ratings and comments are collected. They have also acquired a framework for comparing teaching and courses by attending classes taught by a variety of other instructors, both concurrently and over many preceding years, and from discussing and comparing their experiences with other students (Arreola, 1994).

Many higher education institutions also provide a formal process of peer review, in which a colleague observes a class and discusses their findings with the instructor after the class has concluded. Such feedback can be a useful supplement to SETs information, especially in relation to such matters as the instructor's knowledge of course content. However, peer reviews cover only one class, this class may not be fully representative since the instructor normally knows when their colleague will be attending, and the post-class discussion may not be completely frank if the review process is reciprocal, or friendship is involved.

Most instructors value their professionalism and examine carefully all their ratings and comments. A typical approach to the receipt of SET outputs was outlined by Vanderbilt's Emeritus Professor of Psychology, Kathleen Hoover-Dempsey (who was also a recipient of the university's highest teaching honour, a Chair of Teaching Excellence). During an interview, she stated "I read every comment and find the comments extremely useful in thinking about and improving my own teaching… Overall, I think the numerical ratings are really important, but you often need to analyse students' comments in order to remedy some of the concerns that may underlie lower ratings." (Vanderbilt, 2021).

A second benefit for the more conscientious and better teachers is that their superior performance is made known to administration, which can take the student feedback into account when making decision about promotion and pay.

Analysis of the usefulness of SETs outputs relate mainly to their reliability (internal consistency) and validity (accuracy). Reliability does not seem to be a major concern among researchers. There are, however, vigorous debates about their validity.

Studies conducted prior to the 1990s suggested that SET ratings were reasonably valid measures of teaching effectiveness, with the latter variable generally being measured by end-of-period exam results. For example, a major study by Cohen (1981) showed a correlation of 0.43 between ratings and student performance in common final exams in multisectional classes. Also, Marsh (1987) found that:

> "Ratings are 1) multidimensional; 2) reliable and stable; 3) primarily a function of the instructor who teaches the course rather than the course that is taught; 4) relatively valid against a variety of indicators of effective teaching; 5) relatively unaffected by a variety of variables hypothesised as potential biases; and 6) seen to be useful by faculty …" (Marsh, 1987)

Later studies noted that some of the research undertaken in the 1960s through the 1980s involved researchers who worked for or had been funded by companies developing and selling SET instruments and that this would likely have influenced their results. Other studies have observed that both instructor and course ratings tend to be lower (less favourable) for classes that are small and for courses that are in the hard sciences, are core (versus elective), are out-of-major, and are entry-level. However, the differences in most cases are small (Theall, 2002). Studies have also shown a positive correlation between ratings and grades, and critics of the SETs mechanism have suggested that this could be due to instructors deliberately providing higher grades in the expectation that students will reward them with higher ratings. Since grades are not announced until after the exams are graded, this is problematic. It is just as likely that better teachers both get higher SET scores and produce more learning, with the latter generating the higher grades.

Of more concern is biases relating to race and gender. Skin colour should have no effect on teaching ability, but American studies show that teachers who are white tend to get higher teacher ratings than those of darker complexion. Instructors who are black receive the lowest ratings. Studies on the role of gender are inconclusive, with some studies showing that male students tend to give higher ratings to male instructors and female students tend to provide higher ratings to female instructors, and situational factors (such as female instructors having relatively more large, entry-level courses) explaining some lower ratings for female instructors.

Research also indicates that popularity leads to higher ratings. This is more of a concern for those who feel that student satisfaction is not an appropriate goal, or that popularity detracts from student learning. Further, some instructors might be popular because they are good teachers. Just as researchers funded by SET companies will tend to produce results that favour a strong, positive relationship between teacher ratings and student learning and satisfaction, so researchers like Marilley who claim that "New evidence must be found to overturn the view that evaluations reveal who really knows how to teach …" (Marilley, 1998) will tend to find evidence that casts doubt on the validity of positive ratings.

SETs and administrators

Administrators (such as faculty deans and program directors) use SET ratings as an input into decisions about curricula and courses and about hiring, promotion, tenure, merit-increases. and training for instructors. Well-managed institutions also use many other sources of input, such as consultation with industry bodies and reviews of offerings by competing providers for courses, and recommendations by program managers for matters affecting instructors. Capable deans regard SET ratings as only one of many indicators of teaching performance.

Some researchers claim that many deans rely solely on SET ratings and that because the latter are imperfect, they should be abolished (Stroebe, 2016). This approach would leave some deans with no information, and others with less information, on which to base decisions. A better approach would be to work on organisational structure, recruitment, and training at the managerial level and widen the types of information available to mangers when they are making decisions about employment details of instructors.

RECOMMENDATIONS

1. Like every other educational, psychological, or sociological instrument, SET ratings are imperfect, and should not be sole inputs to policy decisions affecting students, courses, and instructors. They should, however, be one of the inputs.

2. The institutional person that interacts with students during the SETs data collection process should not be the class instructor. Using a person from administration increases the trust of students in the anonymity of the evaluation process.

3. Data should be collected from students during a regular class when attendance is expected to be high (e.g., commencing 30 minutes into the revision class at the end of the trimester). Sufficient time (e.g., 20 minutes) should be allowed so students can think carefully about their ratings and comments.

4. Special attention should be paid to increasing student participation of online students in the SET process, which tends to be about half the rate for onsite students (Vanderbilt, 2021).

5. The person administering the survey should explain to students the importance of the evaluations, especially for future students. They should emphasise that the surveys are confidential, that only summary information will be made available to the instructor, and that this information will not be available until all assessments for the course have been completed.

6. The personalised SET results should be provided to each instructor as soon as possible after student assessments have been finalised and preferably before the start of the following trimester.

7. When evaluating feedback, instructors should take into account both their own situation and the course characteristics. They need to be aware that SET scores tend to be slightly lower for large classes in courses that are quantitative, entry-level, and out-of-major.

8. Instructors should beware of outliers. In very large classes there will always be a generous angel and an angry devil. A well-loved dean at Nottingham University used to advise

new staff that it is not unusual to see a comment like "Professor X is by far the best teacher I have ever had. I wish he/she could deliver all the courses here." followed by "I have never been so bored in my entire life. Time literally stands still during his/her classes" Rather, pay attention to the most frequently mentioned areas for improvement. For new instructors, this will often require providing more time for student participation.

9. Instructors should discuss their evaluations with a trusted colleague. Studies indicate that instructors who do this are more likely to receive higher SET scores in the following teaching period.

10. Instructors and administrators should be trained in the correct interpretation and appropriate use of SET data. A study by Theall and Franklin (1989) showed a strong correlation between both the ability to interpret relevant statistical data and knowledge of common differences and positive attitudes toward the use of SETs for evaluation purposes.

11. Administrators should use SET ratings as only one input into the evaluation process for courses and instructors.

12. The number of questions should be limited to ensure appropriate focus and maximise completion rates.

13. When size permits, higher education providers should consider establishing a Centre for Teaching Excellence that provides general and individual support on course design, delivery, and assessments.

REFERENCES

Arreola, R. (1994). *Developing a Comprehensive Faculty Evaluation System*. Boston: Anker.

Cohen, P. (1981). *Student Ratings of Instruction and Student Achievement: A Meta-analysis of Multisection Validity Studies*. Review of Educational Research.

Theall, M, and Franklin, J. (2002) *Looking for Bias in All the Wrong Places: A Search for Truth or a Witch Hunt in Student Ratings of Instruction? https://onlinelibrary.wiley.com/doi/abs/10.1002/*

Marilley, S. (1998). *Response to 'Colloquy'*. Chronicle of Higher Education.

Marsh, H. (1987*). Students' Evaluations of University Teaching: Research Findings, Methodological Issues, and Directions for Future Research*. International Journal of Educational Research.

Stroebe, W. (2016). *Student Evaluations of Teaching Encourages Poor Teaching and Contributes to Grade Inflation: A Theoretical and Empirical Analysis.*
www.tandfonline.com/doi/full/10.1080/01973533.2020.1756817

Vanderbilt (2021). *Student Evaluations of Teaching.*
https://www.vanderbilt.edu/course-teaching-evaluations/evaluation_reevaluation

Chapter

17

Exploring the Value Creation Link

Richard Xi, Universal Business School Sydney

ABSTRACT (GENERAL SECTION TITLE)

Knowledge and intellectual capital are key resources driving the knowledge economy. Organisations are seeking to gain a competitive advantage and improve their business performance by increasing their knowledge and enhancing their intellectual capabilities in an ever-changing business environment. However, how to effectively utilise and leverage knowledge and intellectual capital to maximise organisational value is a constant challenge for management. This chapter reviews and discusses the dimensions of intellectual capital, the key components of the knowledge management system, the dynamic interactions among these, and the roles they play in creating value within organisations.

INTRODUCTION

With the transition from the Industrial era (1800-2000) to the Digital era (from 2000), economies are moving away from heavy dependence on physical assets such as natural resources, labour, and machinery towards greater reliance on intangible assets such as knowledge and intellectual capital (Powell & Snellman, 2004; OECD, 2005). Knowledge is the most important business resource in a knowledge-based economy (Drucker, 1993). The key components of the knowledge economy – intellectual capital and innovation - are both tied to, and originate from, knowledge. They are the key mediating variables between knowledge (the independent variable) and economic growth (the dependent variable) (see Fig. 1 below). They allow companies to gain a competitive advantage, thereby increasing revenue, containing costs, and creating organisational value. Business leaders "seek to shape and position the organisation's assets, driving forces and activities to remain competitive" (Wiig, 1997, p 399). The ability of companies to gain competitive advantage and create value is determined mainly by their ability to manage knowledge.

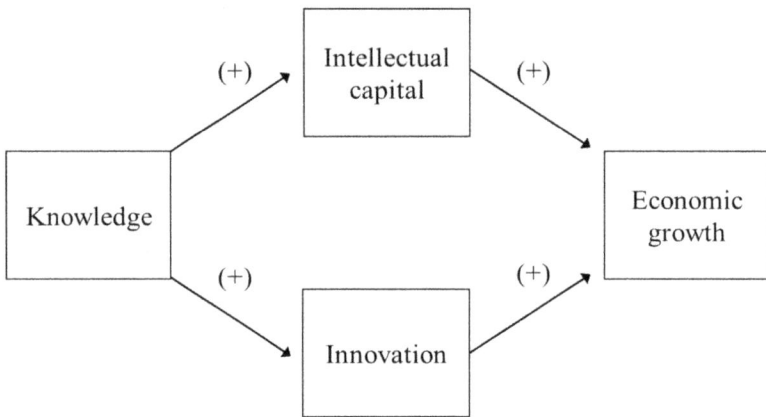

Figure 13 - (Source - Richard Xi 2021)

INTELLECTUAL CAPITAL AND ITS THREE DIMENSIONS

Intellectual capital

There is no agreed definition of intellectual capital (IC) among academics. Stewart (1997) considered it to be intellectual material - such as knowledge, information, intellectual property, and experience - that can be used to create wealth. Investopedia (2021) defined it as the value of the organisation's employee knowledge, skills, business training, and proprietary information that provide it with a competitive advantage. Nahapiet and Ghoshal (1998) referred to it as "the knowledge and knowing capability of a social collectivity, such as an organisation, intellectual community, or professional practice". Focusing on the organization itself, Edvinsson and Malone (1997) defined IC as the sum of human and structural capital, which together encompass the applied experience, organisational technology, customer relationships, and professional skills that provide a company with a competitive advantage in the marketplace.

However, while not identical, these views on IC have some common elements including information, knowledge, and collective knowing capability. IC enables organisations to gain competitive advantage, improve business performance, and create company value. It does this by enhancing business activities such as strategy formulation, innovation, technical development, and management.

Edvinsson (1997), developer of the Scandia model, started with the proposition that the value of a company is ultimately determined by the market. However, the market value of a company is normally greater than the book value (the sum of all the measurable, net tangible assets of the company) as determined by the application of traditional accounting methods. This difference represents the company's IC (Dalkir, 2017). It is a 'hidden' asset, having no monetary presence on the financial statements and reports that have been prepared by the company. However, it truly exists as part of the company's assets and this monetary value is recognised by the market. Developing this 'hidden value' is an important challenge for organisations seeking to create wealth.

The three dimensions of IC and the value creation link

It is common practice to divide an organisation's IC into three categories (or dimensions): human capital (HC), organisational (or structural) capital (OC), and relational (or customer) capital (RC) (Edvinsson & Malone, 1997; Marr, 2008; IFAC in CIMA n.d. P.7). As described by Edvinsson (1997):

- HC covers mostly people's knowledge and skills, know-how, work-related experience, competencies, creativity, and entrepreneurial spirit.

- OC encompasses mainly corporate culture and management philosophy, organisational processes, information systems, trade secrets, trademarks, patents, and copyrights.
- RC includes the organisation's formal and informal relationships (internal and external), customer loyalty and engagement, distribution channels, brand names, corporate reputation, business collaborations, and licensing agreements.

HC is embedded in people's minds. It is the knowledge (most of which is tacit, such as personal know-how, insights, understandings, and experiences) and skills the employee uses to perform their tasks individually or collectively to achieve the organisation's goals. It can be gained from formal/informal education/training and/or accumulated from working, learning, and social experiences. Knowledge is at the centre of the IC platform. It is a key resource in managing the company's routine business activities. It also plays an important role in developing creativity, innovation, and an entrepreneurial spirit, all of which are vital for organisations seeking to gain a competitive edge, create value, and generate wealth in a changing business environment.

OC refers to the structure, systems, and culture of an organisation. From Marr's (2008) viewpoint, OC includes the organisation's corporate values and management philosophy, its processes and routines, and its intellectual property (e.g., patents, copyrights, and trademarks). Edvinsson and Malone (1997) described structural capital as what remains in the organisation after all the people are removed. It includes the company's process capital and innovation capital. OC determines the quantity and quality of the HC (such as know-how and skills) used in performing the routine tasks of the organisation. However, OC can also foster another critical aspect of knowledge – people's attitudes – by developing and nurturing a cultural environment that promotes creativity and innovation. An organisation's innovation capital is a component of OC (Edvinsson and Malone, 1997). It is initiated by people's new and creative ideas based on their knowledge, experience, intuition, attitude, and other knowing-ability (HC elements) and is facilitated and institutionalised by corporate culture and management philosophy

(OC elements). The relationships (connections, interactions, and influence) between HC and OC are particularly important in the process of creating organisational value through innovation.

RC comprises all the internal and external relationships that an organisation holds with its customers. It includes customer loyalty, brand images, business collaborations, distribution channels, and social networks. It is the final component in the IC value creation chain, ensuring that the company's products and services satisfy customers' needs, and therefore create value for the company. Value creation cannot occur in the absence of effective and efficient RC and its successful integration with HC and OC. Consequently, RC plays a pivotal role in the process of translating IC into market value.

KNOWLEDGE AND KNOWLEDGE MANAGEMENT

"We now know that the source of wealth is something specifically human: knowledge. If we apply knowledge to tasks we already know how to do, we call it "productivity." If we apply knowledge to tasks that are new and different, we call it "innovation." Only knowledge allows us to achieve those two goals." (Drucker 2000, p. 96)

The knowledge management concept

Since knowledge is the driving force of economic growth and wealth creation, its acquisition and exploitation have become important objectives for organizations striving to achieve sustainable competitive advantage and business success. Hence, the ability to manage knowledge has become crucial in today's knowledge economy (Dalkir, 2017). With knowledge management (KM) developing into a cross-disciplinary field - ranging from anthropology, management science, information technology, and organizational behaviour to cognitive science and sociology - there is currently no consensus on its definition. Jashapara (2011, p.14) defined it as "the effective learning processes associated with exploration, exploitation and sharing of human knowledge (tacit and explicit) that use appropriate technology and cultural environments to enhance an organisation's intellectual capital and performance." From a business management perspective, KM can be considered as either an organisational strategy or a systematic process for leveraging knowledge to gain a competitive edge and increase organisational value.

However, it is not sufficient just to possess knowledge. As Dalkir (2017, p.2) points out, "Knowledge is abundant, but the ability to use it is scarce." Efficient and effective KM can lift business performance and act as a catalyst for the innovation of new products and services, which is a key to business prosperity and sustainability (Liu, 2020). The argument that 'If knowledge is power, then KM must be even more powerful' reflects the intrinsic value of KM. The latter converts knowledge into power and uses this power to create economic and business value.

The knowledge management process and the value creation link

Notwithstanding that there are various KM process models, developed from different perspectives (e.g., different industries and different types of business), the KM process should be considered, from a holistic view, as an open, integrated system that incorporates key environmental elements (corporate culture and information technology).

The KM model has five stages. Since the activities in each stage interact with and are influenced by activities in other stages, the effectiveness of the process and the quality of the outputs at each stage are crucial to the effectiveness and quality of the output at succeeding stages. For example, the quality of output from Stage 1, 'Knowledge identification and acquisition' should be the 'right' knowledge before it enters Stage 2, 'Knowledge maintenance and organisation'. In turn, this correct knowledge should be maintained and organised properly so that it can provide the most value when it enters Stage 3, 'Knowledge sharing, transferring, and dissemination' – i.e., giving the right knowledge to the right person, in the right place, and at the right time.

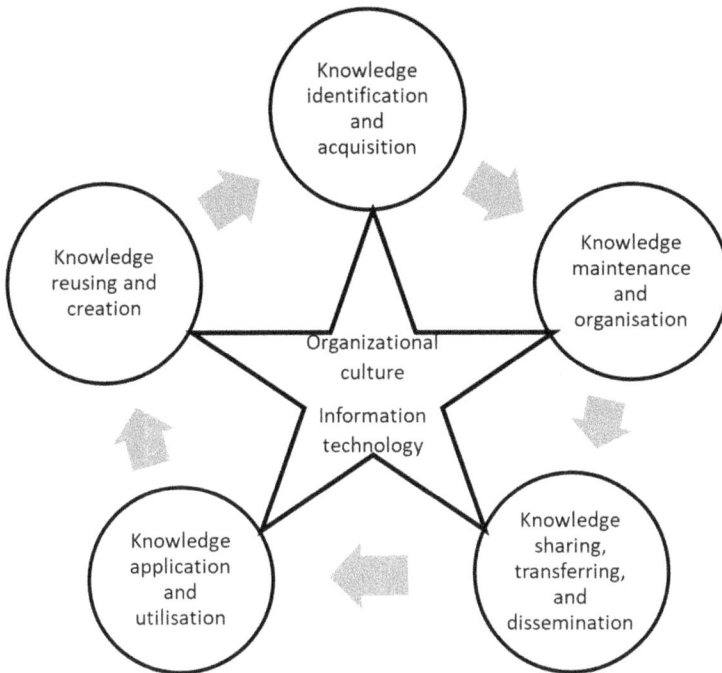

Figure 14 - The open integrated KM model (OIKM)

Further, the success of value creation from the KM processes is also significantly impacted by the synergy among these processes. Finally, whether taking the KM system as a whole or viewing KM as a set of processes, the overall outcome is greatly shaped by the KM environment, particularly the organisational culture, and information technology.

The first stage in the KM process comprises identifying what knowledge the organisation needs (the right knowledge), seeking that knowledge (knowledge exploitation and exploration), and acquiring the knowledge (from either inside of and/or outside of the organisation). The second stage, - maintaining and organising knowledge - covers the processes of analysing, classifying, and storing the gained knowledge (where the dimensions of knowledge include marketing knowledge, management knowledge, and financial knowledge), generally with the support of information technology. Then, the knowledge is ready to go to the third stage – that of sharing, transferring, and disseminating. While explicit knowledge (mainly documents) can be easily articulated, shared, and disseminated, doing so is more complicated and challenging for tacit knowledge (which resides in people's minds). However, tacit knowledge (e.g., know-how, understanding, intuition, attitude, and experience) is the more valuable component of HC. Acquiring, sharing, and disseminating tacit knowledge requires its own set of specific knowledge and skills, and it is a continuing challenge for organisations to acquire, maintain, and develop these. The fourth stage is the application and utilisation of knowledge to realise value for the organisation. In the fifth and final stage, all inputs, processes, and outputs from the four earlier stages are assessed, leading to knowledge reusing (for best practices) and creation (lessons learned, new ideas and new ways of doing things occur, and innovations on the horizon).

CONCLUSION

Knowledge and intellectual capital (IC) are key resources for organisations seeking to obtain a competitive advantage in order to create value and generate wealth in the knowledge economy. However, the conversion of knowledge into real 'power' (ability to create value) and sustaining a profitable return from IC are complicated and challenging tasks for organisations. Having examined and reviewed the key elements of the IC with their subtle relationships embedded in the fabric of HC, OC, and RC, and worked through the processes of the KM system with their dynamic interactions between components and stages, it is suggested that important value-creation links do exist between knowledge, IC and KM and among the elements and components of IC and KM. Achieving the organisational goal of value creation is determined not only by the amount of IC and knowledge, but also by the intellectual capability of the organisation to manage this knowledge.

REFERENCES

CIMA (n.d.). *Understanding corporate value: managing and reporting intellectual capital.*
https://www.cimaglobal.com/Documents/ImportedDocuments/intellectualcapital. Viewed 10 September 2021.

Dalkir, K. (2017). *Knowledge Management in Theory and Practice.* 3rd Edition, The MIT Press, London.

Drucker P.F. (1993). *Post Capitalist Society.*
http://pinguet.free.fr/drucker93.pdf viewed 4 September 2021.

Drucker P. F. (2000). *The Ecological Vision, Reflections on the American Condition.* Transaction Publishers, New Brunswick and London.

Edvinsson, L. and Malone, M. S. (1997). *Intellectual Capital: Realizing Your Company's True Value* by Finding its Hidden Brainpower. Judy Piatkus (Publishers) Ltd, London.

Investopedia,
https://www.investopedia.com/terms/i/intellectual_capital.asp viewed 2 September 2021.

Jashapara A. (2011), *Knowledge Management an Integrated Approach.* 2nd Edition, Pearson Education Limited, England.

Liu S. (2020). *Knowledge Management: An interdisciplinary approach for business decisions.* Kogan Page Limited, London.

Marr B. (2008). *Impacting Future Value: How to Manage Your Intellectual Capital*
https://www.cimaglobal.com/Documents/ImportedDocuments/tech_mag_impactingfuturevalue_may08.pdf.pdf viewed 2 September 2021.

Nahapiet, J. and Ghoshal, S. (1998), *Social capital, intellectual capital, and the organizational advantage.* Academy of Management Review, Vol. 23, No. 2, pp. 242-266.

OECD (2005), *Knowledge-based Economy.*
https://stats.oecd.org/glossary/detail.asp?ID=6864 viewed 4 September 2021.

Powell W. and Snellman K. (2004). *The Knowledge Economy*
https://www.researchgate.net/publication/234838566_The_Knowledge_Economy/link/0f317533c8be33a61d000000/download viewed 4 September 2021.

Stewart, T. A. (1997), *Intellectual Capital: The New Wealth of Organizations*. Doubleday/Currency, New York.

Wiig K. M. (1997) *Integrating Intellectual Capital and Knowledge Management*. Long Range Planning, Vol. 30, No. 3, pp. 399-405.

Chapter

18

Diversity, Business Objectives, and Education

Jotsana Roopram, Universal Business School Sydney

Angus Hooke, Universal Business School Sydney

Greg Whateley, Universal Business School Sydney

ABSTRACT

Support for the view that the primary objective of companies should be to maximise the wealth of shareholders is based on the Adam Smith principle that the best way for a person to promote the social interest is to pursue their self-interest. However, companies are increasingly being asked to add a range of secondary objectives, mainly concerned with diversity, equity, and the environment. Some proponents of the broader approach maintain that they are not challenging the traditional business model, and that the secondary objectives are effectively mediating variables that facilitate the maximisation of profits and shareholder wealth. The authors of this Chapter develop a model to help analyse some of the effects of one secondary objective – greater diversity – on economic welfare. They also consider how one education provider in Sydney has addressed the challenge of achieving optimum diversity among its students.

INTRODUCTION

Adam Smith, the "father of capitalism" argued that the best guide for people seeking to promote the social interest is to pursue their own interests. Smith believed that this principle applied to workers, consumers, and investors: in most situations, activities aimed at maximising own welfare also maximise social welfare (Smith, 1776).

Economists have since constructed theoretical models to demonstrate that, if (1) producers and consumers have full and accurate knowledge of production and consumption possibilities (perfect knowledge), (2) there are no externalities of production or consumption (full appropriability), and (3) markets are competitive, then Smith is correct. They have further demonstrated that these conditions are largely met for about 80% of activity in free-market economies. This has led to widespread support for the view that the private sector, motivated by self-interest (referred to as rational behaviour), should take care of that part of economic activity where the above conditions prevail, and governments should look after the remaining 20%. This, in turn, has led to the view that the primary objective of business firms (responsible for the 80%) should be to maximise the wealth of owners. For companies, where ownership is largely divorced from operations, the primary objective of the directors (the agents) should be to maximise the wealth of the shareholders (the principals), generally by maximising profits.

In the middle of the 20th century, when memories of the decade-long Great Depression and the half-decade-long World War II were still crystal clear and exceedingly painful, corporate social responsibility (CSR) was largely synonymous with maximising shareholder wealth. Since then, real gross world product (GWP) has increased 12-fold and real per capita income has risen 4-fold. This increase in prosperity has been accompanied by a widening of the scope of many people's understanding of CSR to include a range of secondary objectives, mostly social and environmental.

While some hold the view that our higher income should be spread across a wider range of benefits, others suggest that the secondary objectives are simply compensating for imperfect knowledge on the part of producers about the capability of historically marginalised groups (MacRae, 2021). They are, therefore, consistent with the traditional, free enterprise approach - policies aimed at increasing diversity and equity and at improving the environment can reduce knowledge imperfections in the labour and product markets, thereby increasing profits and, through this mechanism, also increasing social welfare. This Chapter has two aims: first, to construct and apply a framework for analysing the effect of one proposed secondary objective (increased diversity) on economic welfare (the contribution by economic activity to total welfare): and secondly, to describe how one higher education provider, Universal Business School Sydney (UBSS) has successfully incorporated diversity into its business model.

THE MODEL

General assumptions

The model assumes that:

1. The work force is divided evenly between two groups - those born in Australia (W_{AUS}) and those born in New Zealand (W_{NZ})
2. The wage rate in the target industry is the same for all members of both groups
3. Due to differences in business-relevant knowledge and skills, the marginal labour productivity (MLP) of members within both groups is subject to diminishing marginal returns
4. There are no work-relevant differences between the two groups. The MLP schedules for both W_{AUS} and W_{NZ} are not only downward sloping, they are also identical; and
5. Those responsible for making decisions about new hires have correct perceptions about the MLP of W_{AUS} but, initially, they underestimate the MLP of W_{NZ}.

Initial situation – inefficient allocation of labour

Fig. 15 describes this initial situation. The MLP curves for W_{AUS} and W_{NZ} are shown on the left-hand and right-hand axes, respectively. Employment is shown on the horizontal axis, with W_{AUS} measured to the right from the left-vertical axis and W_{NZ} measured to the left from the right-vertical axis. The horizontal base line therefore shows total employment. AB is the MLP curve for W_{AUS}. CD is the actual MLP curve for W_{NZ} and C_1D_1 is the perceived MLP curve for W_{NZ}. Equilibrium employment is at E, where the actual MLP curve for W_{AUS} intersects with the perceived

MLP curve for W_{NZ}. The diagram illustrates that the actual MLP of W_{NZ} is higher than the actual MLP of W_{AUS}. This results in a deadweight loss (the loss to society due to an inefficient allocation of resources) equal to the area of the shaded triangle JKH.

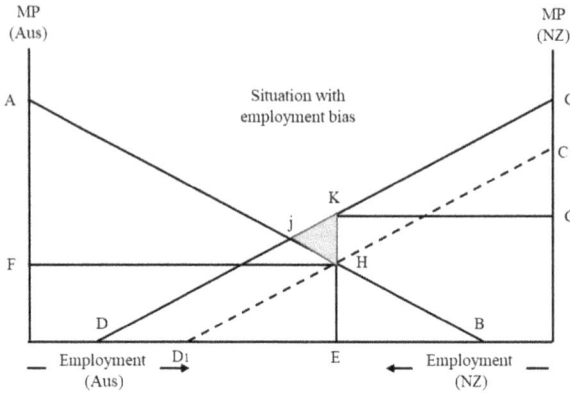

Figure 15 - MLP curves, inefficient allocation of labour

Disturbance

Now suppose that the employment bias against W_{NZ} is removed. This could happen because those making hiring decisions acquire the ability to correctly assess the capability of W_{NZ}. It could also be due to an intervention such as the introduction of a quota that, fortuitously, predicts the economically efficient employment of W_{NZ}.

New situation – efficient allocation of labour

The new situation is illustrated in Fig. 16. Equilibrium employment moves to the left, to E_1, with EE_1 New Zealand born workers replacing the same number of Australian born workers. As this occurs, the MLP of New Zealand born workers declines (from EK to E_1J) and that of Australian born workers increases (from EH to E_1J). The process stops when the MLPs of New Zealand born, and Australian born workers are equal.

MP
(Aus)

MP
(NZ)

A

Situation without
employment bias

C

K

j

F₁

G₁

F

H

D

B

E₁ E

Employment
(Aus)

Employment
(NZ)

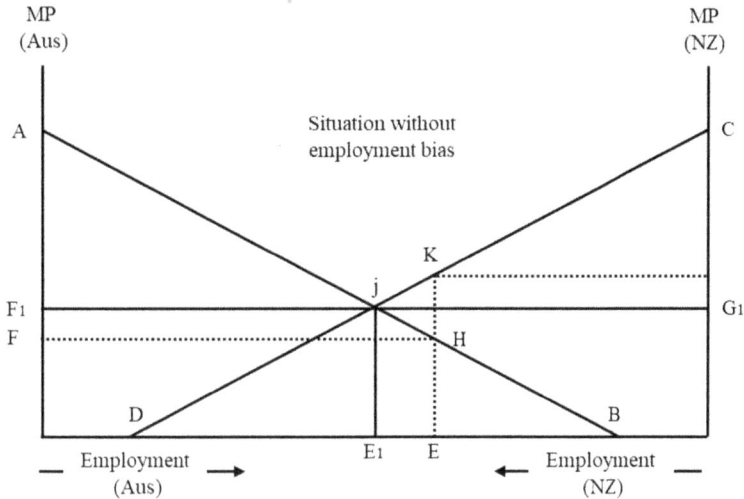

Figure 16 - MLP curves, efficient allocation of labour

THE RESPONSES

The model depicts a situation in which the substitution of workers whose economic worth had not been fully recognised (W_{NZ}) for other workers who were less productive resulted in an increase in welfare. This desirable outcome raises two questions: (1) how to identify the labour force misallocations; and (2) how to correct them. Many groups claim to be discriminated against based on gender, age, race, ethnicity, appearance, family relationships, and the like. Assessing their claims is complex and is beyond the scope of this chapter. We will, however, briefly address the responses issue, considering two approaches, namely, (1) the adoption of quotas that prescribe an employment outcome in advance; and (2) the provision of education and training to overcome the knowledge imperfection that gave rise to the initial discrimination.

Quotas

This is an interventionist approach, generally favoured by those on the left side of politics. It involves companies setting a target for employment of those in the disadvantaged group, most commonly reflecting their size in the total population or a relevant subset of the population. For example, following the model above, if 10% of the population were born in New Zealand, the targeted Australian companies should ensure that 10% of their own work forces were born in New Zealand.

The strong advantage of quotas is that they can lead to quick changes. Management simply advises the HR department that, say, of the 20 positions to be filled in the following month, four appointees must meet the condition that they were born in New Zealand. If the only form of disadvantage being considered is country of birth, if the quota correctly identifies the economically efficient number of New Zealand born employees, and if that number does not change over time, then the problem can be fixed quickly and easily.

The weaknesses of quotas include the slippery-slope phenomenon and quota rigidity. If the employment opportunities being considered are attractive, such as membership of an executive board or positions in senior management, other groups that feel disadvantaged may also join in the quest for quotas, producing an administrative burden. Further, even if only one special interest group is seeking quota support, the quota number that is appropriate at one point in time will probably not be the correct number for long, making the quota itself a source of inefficiency and disadvantage. A measure designed to remove disadvantage and improve efficiency in the short run can easily lock-in inefficiency in the long run.

Education and training

This is the free market approach, strongly favoured by the conservatives on the political right. If the inefficiency is caused by lack of knowledge, then education and training can be used to remove the imperfection. The advantage of the approach is that it retains the decentralised decision-making strength of the free-market economy, allowing companies to consider all differences among job applicants (e.g., intelligence, education levels, experience, and communication skills). The main disadvantage is that changing the way key decision-makers think can be a slow process (e.g., for racial and ethnic discrimination) and time may be a limiting resource if the issue of disadvantage has become politically very sensitive. However, this approach will generally lead to economically correct outcomes over the longer term.

THE UBSS APPROACH TO DIVERSITY

In 2016, UBSS developed a strategic plan. Although it has revisited the plan on several occasions, the fundamental structure has remained intact with five pillars underlying the growth and development of the business – a higher education provider with a focus on international students primarily but with an appetite for domestic students. The latest iteration, (2020-2022), was created in late 2019, and supported by the GCA Board of Directors (GCA Board, 2021).

The five pillars comprise growth, diversity, quality, entrepreneurship, and benchmarking. At the very core of the foci is student participation and attainment – which in turn leads to reputation, profile, and profit. A close examination of the diversity focus provides a valuable insight into the elements of diversity (closely linked with the quality pillar) - measured and reported against on a regular (at least monthly) basis. Diversity is defined, contextualised, and explained from the outset (pp 9 and 10).

"Diversity tells us about who we are. Diversity provides our students with a truly international community on which we overlay a quality Australian educational experience. UBSS has an international student focus, but our intention is to grow our domestic opportunities appropriately. Source countries tell us about ourselves and energise our recruitment and marketing strategy. The balance of undergraduate and post graduate students is also an important part of our make-up. The Measures form the KPIs against which we are able to monitor and report our progress." (GCA Board, 2021)

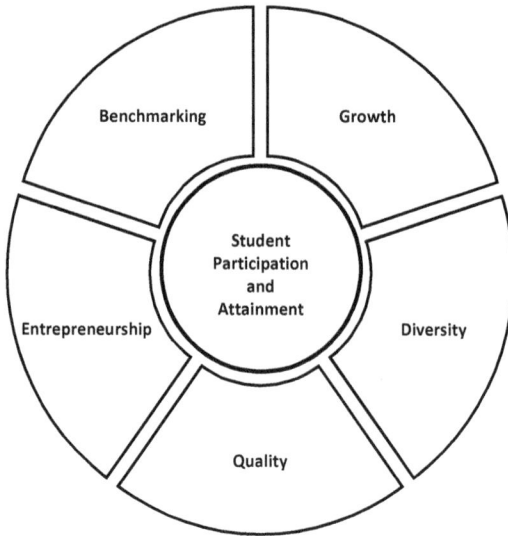

Figure 17 - The UBSS approach to diversity

The strategies envisaged to ensure diversity are made clear:

- Improve our widening participation profile, while maintaining entry standards
- Enhance our postgraduate offerings and increase uptake – both internationally and domestically
- Capitalise on our investments in information systems and tools
- Develop our learning and teaching infrastructure, technology systems and processes
- Develop graduates who are engaged; enterprising and enquiring; ethically, globally, are culturally aware; and have the skills, knowledge, and entrepreneurial spirit to progress their careers and engage with societal challenges; and
- Maintain an operating surplus sufficient to meet our strategic aims in a financially sustainable manner.

UBSS recognises that appropriate diversity produces better outcomes:

Good schools encourage diversity. Excellent schools energise diversity and develop a range of activities that maximise quality and opportunity (GCA Board, 2021).

Diversity and student cohorts

Table 10 - KPIs on the diversity of UBSS student cohorts

	2019	2020	2021	2022
Domestic	8	178	433	433
Executive	8	138	333	333
Virtual	0	40	100	100
International	1600	1844	2242	2393
Sydney	1600	1600	1600	1600
Melbourne	0	200	350	500
Virtual	0	44	292	292
Nationalities	30	30	30	30
Countries with 10 +	10	10	10	10
Undergraduate (%)	50	47	43	40
Postgraduate (%)	50	53	57	60

Note. The COVID-19 pandemic has had a significant impact on projections, but UBSS remains confident that these same outcomes can be achieved by end 2024.

The succinct, well thought through diversity plan provides a focus for all staff members at UBSS around student recruitment and management. For UBSS, this diversity is essential to achieve not only growth, but heightened levels of student satisfaction with the learning experience.

CONCLUSION

Diversity promotes creativity, tolerance, empathy, and understanding. Like other Australian higher education providers, UBSS seeks to achieve optimal diversity among both staff and students. Its success in this area is being reflected in happy working and learning environments, high levels of productivity among staff, and very pleasing academic performance by students.

REFERENCES

GCA Board, (2021). *UBSS Strategic Plan 2020 to 2022 - https://www.ubss.edu.au/media/1746/strategic-plan-v9.pdf*

MacRae, D. (2021). *Toward Benevolent AGI by Integrating Knowledge Graphs for Classical Economics, Education, and Health.* In Technological Breakthroughs and Future Business Opportunities in Education, Health, and Outer Space. IGI Global.

Smith, A, (1776). *An Enquiry into the Nature and Causes of the Wealth of Nations.* The University of Chicago Press.

Compilation of References

Reference	Ch
Abed, S. 2014. *A review of e-accounting education for undergraduate accounting degrees.* Int. Bus. Res., 7: 113-119.	7
Abeysekera, L. and Dawan P. (2015*), Motivation and cognitive load in the flipped classroom: definition, rational and a call for research,* Higher Education Research & Development 34(1): 1-14.	9
Accenture (2021) *Communications and media technology Vision 2020* Retrieved from *https://www.accenture.com/us-en/insights/communications-media/technology-vision*	11
Afterpay, (2021). *https://www.afterpay.com/en-US/for-retailers*	3
Aguinis, H., Forcum, L. E., & Joo, H. (2012). *Using Market Basket Analysis in Management Research.* Journal of Management. doi:10.1177/0149206312466147.	1
APH (2021). *Overseas students in Australian higher education: a quick guide* Updated 22 April 2021. *https://www.aph.gov.au/About_Parliament/Parliamentary_Depa rtments/Parliamentary_Library/pubs/rp/rp2021/Quick_Guides /OverseasStudents,* viewed 25th September, 2021.	14
Arreola, R. (1994). *Developing a Comprehensive Faculty Evaluation System.* Boston: Anker.	16
Australian Government, Department of Education, *Skills and Employment.* (2021) Retrieved from *https://internationaleducation.gov.au/regulatory-information/Education-Services-for-Overseas-Students-ESOS-Legislative-Framework/National-Code/Pages/default*	13
Autor, D.H. (2015). *Why Are There Still So Many Jobs? The History and Future of Workplace Automation.* Journal of Economic Perspectives. Vol. 29, No. 3, Summer. Pp. 3-30.	4

Reference	Ch
Ballard, B. and Chandry, J. (1991). *Teaching Students from Overseas: A Brief Guide for Lecturers and Supervisors*, Longman Cheshire, Sydney.	7
Baron, P. & Corbin, L. (2012). *Student engagement: rhetoric and reality.* Higher Education Research & Development, 31 (6), 759-772.	8
Bateman, T. and Snell, S. (2012). *Management: Leading and Collaborating in the Competitive World*, 10th ed., Australia: McGraw-Hill.	10
Bloom, B. (1956). *Taxonomy of Educational Objectives: The Classification of Educational Goals*, *https://www.google.com/search* accessed on 26/10/21	10
Bowen, S. (2005). *Engaged learning: Are we on the same page?* Peer Review, 7 (2), 4–7.	8
Boyce, G. (1999). *Computer-assisted teaching and learning in accounting: pedagogy or product?*, Journal of Accounting Education, Vol. 17 Nos 2/3, pp. 191-220.	7
Brownlee, J. (2017). *Master Machine Learning Algorithms: Discover How They Work and Implement Them From Scratch.* Melbourne, Australia: Mastery Machine Learning Series.	1
Carey, K (2019). *The Creeping Capitalist Takeover of Higher Education.* Huffpost, *https://www.huffpost.com/highline/article/capitalist-takeover-college/*, viewed 20th September 2021.	14
Carol, J. and Rayan, J. (2005). *Teaching International Students.* Oxon: Routledge	10
Chanda, A. (2021) *The efficacy of online studies.* Retrieved from *https://www.ubss.edu.au/media/2695/the-efficacy-of-online-studies*	11
Chanda, A. (2021) *The efficacy of online studies.* Retrieved from *https://www.ubss.edu.au/media/2695/the-efficacy-of-online-studies*	13

Reference	Ch
Chase, C. (2018). *The Economic Singularity.* *https://www.youtube.com/watch?v=FZh_SzVDQVI*	4
Chavan, M. (2011). *Higher Education Students' Attitudes Towards Experiential Learning in International Business.* Journal of Teaching in International Business, 22, 126–143.	8
Chickering, A. and Gamson, Z. (1987). *Seven Principles for Good Practice in Undergraduate Education.* *https://eric.ed.gov/?id=ed282491*, accessed on 21/10/21	10
CIMA (n.d.). *Understanding corporate value: managing and reporting intellectual capital.* *https://www.cimaglobal.com/Documents/ImportedDocuments/intellectualcapital.* Viewed 10 September 2021.	17
Cohen, P. (1981). *Student Ratings of Instruction and Student Achievement: A Meta-analysis of Multisection Validity Studies.* Review of Educational Research.	16
Cook-Sather, A. and Luz, A. (2015). *Greater engagement in and responsibility for learning: what happens when students cross the threshold of student–faculty partnership.* Higher Education Research & Development, 34(6), 1097-1109.	8
Dalkir, K. (2017). *Knowledge Management in Theory and Practice.* 3rd Edition, The MIT Press, London.	17
Dave, N. (2021). *42 Digital Marketing Trends You Can't Ignore in 2021. https://www.singlegrain.com/digital-marketing/digital-marketing-trends-2021/*	3
Davenport, T. H. (2018). *From analytics to artificial intelligence.* Journal of Business Analytics, 1(2), 73-80. doi:10.1080/2573234x.2018.1543535.	1
De Bruyn, A., Viswanathan, V., Beh, Y. S., Brock, J. K.-U., & von Wangenheim, F. (2020). *Artificial Intelligence and Marketing: Pitfalls and Opportunities.* Journal of Interactive Marketing, 51, 91-105. doi:10.1016/j.intmar.2020.04.007.	2
Deci, E. L., & Ryan, R. M. (1985). *Intrinsic motivation and self-determination in human behaviour.* USA: Plenum Press.	8

Reference	Ch
Diamandis, P. and Kotler, S. (2012. *Abundance: The Future is Better Than You Think*. Free Press.	6
Drucker P. F. (2000). *The Ecological Vision, Reflections on the American Condition*. Transaction Publishers, New Brunswick and London.	17
Drucker P.F. (1993). *Post Capitalist Society*. *http://pinguet.free.fr/drucker93.pdf* viewed 4 September 2021.	17
Drucker, P. (2015). *Innovation and Entrepreneurship*, Routledge. *https://www.routledge.com/Innovation-and-Entrepreneurship/Drucker/p/book/*	3
Edvinsson, L. and Malone, M. S. (1997). *Intellectual Capital: Realizing Your Company's True Value* by Finding its Hidden Brainpower. Judy Piatkus (Publishers) Ltd, London.	17
FAO (2021). *How to feed the world in 2050*. Retrieved from *https://www.fao.org/fileadmin/templates/wsfs/docs/expert*	6
Fitzell, D. J. (1970, Jan 1). *The importance of continuing professional development*. Retrieved from: *http://www.professionalsaustralia.org.au/australian-government/blog/the-importance-of-continuing-professional-development/*	12
Ford, M. (2015). *Rise of the robots: Technology and the threat of a jobless future*. New York: Basic Books.	4
Fox-Jensen, E. (2021). *Collaborative Learning Methods, Tools, Research and Practical Models within a Digital Learning Environment*: Ethics, Caring and Sharing Design,' doi: 10.13140/8622.25308.10881/1.	10
Garrison, D.R. & Vaughan, N.D. (2008), *Blended Learning in Higher Education: Framework, Principles, and guidelines*. San Francisco: Jossey-Bass.	9
Gartner (2021). *Online Program Management in Higher Education*. *https://www.gartner.com/reviews/market/online-program-management-in-higher-education*, viewed 26th September 2021.	14

Reference	Ch
GCA Board, (2021). *UBSS Strategic Plan 2020 to 2022 - https://www.ubss.edu.au/media/1746/strategic-plan-v9.pdf*	18
George, G., Haas, M. R., & Pentland, A. (2014). *Big Data and Management.* Academy of Management Journal, 57(2), 321-326. doi:10.5465/amj.2014.4002.	1
Grönroos, C. (2016). *On defining marketing: finding a new roadmap for marketing.* Marketing Theory, 6(4), 395-417. doi:10.1177/1470593106069930.	2
Hackl, C. (2021). CMO Network. *https://www.forbes.com/sites/cathyhackl/2020/07/05/the-metaverse-is-coming--its-a-very-big-deal/?sh=6e516d38440f*	3
Hare, J (2021). *Online Boom Ahead as Unis Outsource Teaching.* Australian Financial Review, 24 May 2021 edition.	14
Harvard Business Review – *https://hbr.org/2021/03/10-truths-about-marketing-after-the-pandemic*	5
Hill, P (2021). *OPM Market Landscape and Dynamics Summer 2021 Updates. https://philonedtech.com/opm-market-landscape-and-dynamics-summer-2021-updates/*, viewed 25 September 2021.	14
HolonIQ (2021). *244 University Partnerships in the First Half of 2021. https://www.holoniq.com/notes/opm-mooc-opx.-244-university-partnerships-in-the-first-half-of-2021/*, Viewed 24 September 2021.	14
Hooke, A. (2019). *Global Economic Development: Past. Present, and Future.* Lakeland House.	6
Hooke, A. and Alati, L. (2021). *Technological Breakthroughs and Future Business Opportunities in Education, Health, and Outer Space.* IGI Global.	6
Hsu, L., & Chen, Y.-J. (2021). *Neuromarketing, Subliminal Advertising, and Hotel Selection: An EEG Study.* Australasian Marketing Journal, 28(4), 200-208. doi:10.1016/j.ausmj.2020.04.009.	2

Reference	Ch
https://www.ey.com/en_au/consumer-products-retail/how-covid-19-could-change-consumer-behavior	5
https://www.mckinsey.com/business-functions/marketing-and-sales/our-insights/reimagining-marketing-in-the-next-normal	5
https://www.smh.com.au/national/what-goes-wrong-when-uni-students-mark-their-teachers-20210831-p58nk0	15
https://www.smh.com.au/national/what-goes-wrong-when-uni-students-mark-their-teachers-20210831-p58nk0	15
https://www.ubss.edu.au/articles/2021/may/online-teaching-a-tale-of-two-institutions/	15
https://www.ubss.edu.au/articles/2021/may/online-teaching-a-tale-of-two-institutions/	15
https://www.ubss.edu.au/articles/2021/september/alternative-delivery-options/	15
Huang, M.-H., & Rust, R. T. (2020). *A strategic framework for artificial intelligence in marketing.* Journal of the Academy of Marketing Science, 49(1), 30-50. doi:10.1007/s11747-020-00749-9.	2
IBIS World (2021). *Online Shopping in Australia – Market Research Report. https://www.ibisworld.com/au/industry/online-shopping/1837*	3
Investopedia, *https://www.investopedia.com/terms/i/intellectual_capital.asp* viewed 2 September 2021.	17
Israeli, A. (2020). *Digital learning REMOTE a framework for teaching online.* Harvard Business Publishing accessed on 28 February 2021 from *https://hbsp.harvard.edu/inspiring-minds/remote-a-framework-for-teaching-online*	8
Jashapara A. (2011), *Knowledge Management an Integrated Approach.* 2nd Edition, Pearson Education Limited, England.	17

Reference	Ch
Johns Hopkins Center for a Liveable Future (2021). *History of Agriculture.* Retrieved from *https://www.foodsystemprimer.org/food-production/history-of-agriculture*	6
Karasik, R. J. (2012). *Engaged Teaching for Engaged Learning: Sharing Your Passion for Gerontology and Geriatrics,* Gerontology & Geriatrics Education. 33:2, 119-132.	8
Keynes, John Maynard. (1930). *Economic Possibilities for our Grandchildren. https://medium.com/8vc-news/the-future-of-labor-pt-i-keynes-f3ae0f2808b6*	4
Kimakowitz, E. v., Pirson, M., Spitzeck, H., Dierksmeier, C., & Amann, W. (Eds.). (2011). *Humanistic Management in Practice.* London, UK: Palgrave Macmillan.	2
Klebs, S. (et al) (2021) *One year later – COVID-19's impact on current and future college students.* Retrieved from *http://thirdway.imgix.net/pdfs/one-year-later-covid-19s-impact-on-current-and-future-college-students*	13
Kolb, A. Y. & Kolb, D. A. (2010). *Learning to play, playing to learn: A case study of a ludic learning space.* Journal of Organizational Change Management, 23(1), 26-50.	8
Kotler, P., & Keller, K. (2016). *Marketing Management,* 15th edn, Pearson Education, England.	10
Kotler, P., Kartajaya, H., & Setiawan, I. (2016). *Marketing 4.0: Moving from Traditional to Digital.* New York, USA: John Wiley & Sons.	2
Kotler, P., Kartajaya, H., & Setiawan, I. (2021). *Marketing 5.0 Technology for Humanity.* New York, USA: John Wiley & Sons.	2
Kurt, R. (2019). *Industry 4.0 in Terms of Industrial Relations and Its Impacts on Labour Life.* Procedia Computer Science. Volume 158, pp 590-601. *https://doi.org/10.1016/j.procs.2019.09.093*	4

Reference	Ch
Laskow, S. (2017). *A machine that made stockings helped kick off the industrial revolution.* *https://www.atlasobscura.com/articles/machine-silk-stockings-industrial-revolution-queen-elizabeth*	4
Lim, W. M. (2018). *Demystifying neuromarketing.* Journal of Business Research, 91, 205-220. doi:10.1016/j.jbusres.2018.05.036.	2
Lima, Y.; Barbosa, C.E.; dos Santos, H.S.; de Souza, J.M. (2021). *Understanding Technological Unemployment: A Review of Causes, Consequences, and Solutions.* Societies. 11, 50. *https://doi.org/10.3390/soc11020050*	4
Liu S. (2020). *Knowledge Management: An interdisciplinary approach for business decisions.* Kogan Page Limited, London.	17
Llopis, G. (2013). *Forbes, Leadership Strategy.* *https://www.forbes.com/sites/glennllopis/2013/04/01/12-things-successfully-convert-a-great-idea-into-a-reality/?sh=77fb9f024e86*	3
Lytle, R. (2020). *How COVID-19 has impacted higher education in Mexico, Colombia and Peru.* EY-Parthenon Education sector.	12
MacRae, D. (2021). *Toward Benevolent AGI by Integrating Knowledge Graphs for Classical Economics, Education, and Health.* In Technological Breakthroughs and Future Business Opportunities in Education, Health, and Outer Space. IGI Global.	18
Mallik, G., & Shankar, S. (2016). *Does prior knowledge of economics and higher level mathematics improve student learning in principles of economics,* Economic Analysis and Policy, Volume 49, March 2016, Pages 66-73.	9
Manly, A. (2021). *A Simple Plan, Inside Small Business.* *https://insidesmallbusiness.com.au/management/a-simple-plan*	3
Marilley, S. (1998). *Response to 'Colloquy'.* Chronicle of Higher Education.	16

Reference	Ch
Marr B. (2008). *Impacting Future Value: How to Manage Your Intellectual Capital* *https://www.cimaglobal.com/Documents/ImportedDocuments/tech_mag_impactingfuturevalue_may08.pdf.pdf* viewed 2 September 2021.	17
Marsh, H. (1987*). Students' Evaluations of University Teaching: Research Findings, Methodological Issues, and Directions for Future Research.* International Journal of Educational Research.	16
Marshall, S. (2020) *The digital workplace defined* CMS WiRE, Retrieved from *https://www.cmswire.com/cms/social-business/what-a-digital-workplace-is-and-what-it-isnt-027421*	11
McDowall, T. and Jackling, B. (2006). *The impact of computer-assisted learning on academic grades: an assessment of students' perceptions*, Accounting Education: An International Journal, Vol. 15 No. 4, pp. 377-389.	7
Nahapiet, J. and Ghoshal, S. (1998), *Social capital, intellectual capital, and the organizational advantage.* Academy of Management Review, Vol. 23, No. 2, pp. 242-266.	17
National Survey of Student Engagement. (2017). *https://bit.ly/2Kyxkzo*	8
Ng, S. (2021). *Transitioning towards studying online: A reflection. An unpublished write-up by a current post graduate student studying with a private provider in Sydney*, 1-8. Australia.	8
Ng. W., (2015). *New Digital Technology in Education: Conceptualising Professional Learning for Educators.* Springer International Publishing.	9
Noe, R. A., Tews, M. J. and Dachner, A. M. (2010). *Learner Engagement: A New Perspective for Enhancing Our Understanding of Learner Motivation and Workplace Learning.* The Academy of Management Annals, 4(1), 279–315.	8
O'Connor, L. (2021). *https://www.theguardian.com/small-business-network/2015/jul/31/six-ways-become-entreprenuer-business-idea*	3

Reference	Ch
OBERLO statistics (2021). Global e-commerce sales, cited: *https://au.oberlo.com/statistics/global-ecommerce-sales*	3
OECD (2005), *Knowledge-based Economy.* *https://stats.oecd.org/glossary/detail.asp?ID=6864* viewed 4 September 2021.	17
Orton, T and Curry-Hyde, E (2021), *Our Universities Have Been Gold Medallists Before, Here's How they can do it again –* Nous Group. *https://www.nousgroup.com/insights/universities-gold-medallists/*, viewed 2nd October, 2021.	14
Phillips, A. (2021). *Interview Style Guest Presentations that Enhance Learning.* *https://www.ubss.edu.au/media/2785/interview-style-guest-presentations-that-enhance-learning.pdf*	3
PICPA, Articles. (2019, Apr 19). Retrieved from PICPA - Pennsylvania Institute of CPAs: *https://www.picpa.org/articles/picpa-news/2019/04/23/pa-cpa-journal-prepping-accounting-students-for-a-new-tech-world*	12
Powell W. and Snellman K. (2004). *The Knowledge Economy* *https://www.researchgate.net/publication/234838566_The_Knowledge_Economy/link/0f317533c8be33a61d000000/download* viewed 4 September 2021.	17
Price, C., & Walker, M. (2019). *Improving the accessibility of foundation statistics for undergraduate business and management students using a flipped classroom.* Studies in Higher Education, DOI: 10.1080/03075079.2019. 1628204.	9
Quinlan, J. R. (1979). *Discovering rules by induction from large collections of examples.* In D. Michie (Ed.), Expert systems in the micro electronic age. Edinburgh: Edinburgh University Press.	1
Quinlan, J. R. (1993). C4.5: *Programs for machine learning.* San Mateo, USA: Morgan Kaufmann Publishers.	1

Reference	Ch
Reeve, J. (2002). *Self-determination theory applied to educational settings.* In E. L. Deci & R. M. Ryan (Eds.), Handbook of self-determination research, 183–203. NY, USA: University of Rochester Press.	8
Reserve Bank of Australia (2017) *The rising share of part-time employment.* Retrieved from *https://www.rba.gov.au/publications/bulletin/2017/sep/3*	11
Ritter F. E.; et al., eds. (2007). *In order to learn: how the sequence of topics influences learning. Oxford series on cognitive models and architectures.* Oxford/New York: Oxford University Press. ISBN 978-0-19-517884-5.	9
Robbins, S. P., Judge, T., Millett, B. and Boyle, M. (2016). *Organisational behaviour*, 17th edn, USA: Pearson.	8
Ryan, R. M., & Deci, E. L. (2000). *Self-determination theory and the facilitation of intrinsic motivation, social development, and well-being.* American Psychologist, 55 (1), 68–78. *https://doi.org/10.1037/0003-066X.55.1.68*	8
Shantha P. and Shan Y. (2012). *Power of Teaching by Walking Around. https://www.ft.lk/Opinion-and-Issues/power-of-teaching-by-walking-around/14-112876*, accessed on 21/10/21.	10
Simon, H. A. (1967). *The Business School: A Problem In Organizational Design.* The Journal Of Management Studies, 4(1), 1-16.	1
Simsek, Z., Vaara, E., Paruchuri, S., Nadkarni, S., & Shaw, J. D. (2019). *New Ways of Seeing Big Data.* Academy of Management Journal, 62(4), 971-978. doi:10.5465/amj.2019.4004.	1
Smallhorn, M. (2017). *The flipped classroom: A learning model to increase student engagement not academic achievement.* Student Success, B (2), 43-53. DOI: 10.5204/ssj. v8i2.381.	9
Smith, A, (1776). *An Enquiry into the Nature and Causes of the Wealth of Nations.* The University of Chicago Press.	18

Reference	Ch
Spais, G., & Paul, P. (2021). *A Crisis Management Model For Marketing Education: Reflections On Marketing Education System's Transformation In View Of The Covid-19 Crisis.* Marketing Education Review, 1-18.	2
Stasi, A., Songa, G., Mauri, M., Ciceri, A., Diotallevi, F., Nardone, G., & Russo, V. (2018). *Neuromarketing empirical approaches and food choice: A systematic review.* Food Res Int, 108, 650-664. doi:10.1016/j.foodres.2017.11.049.	2
Sterne, J. (2017). *Artificial Intelligence for Marketing: Practical Applications.* New York, NY: John Wiley & Sons.	2
Stewart, T. A. (1997), *Intellectual Capital: The New Wealth of Organizations.* Doubleday/Currency, New York.	17
Strain, J. (2021). *https://www.afterpay.com/en-US/for-retailers*	3
Stroebe, W. (2016). *Student Evaluations of Teaching Encourages Poor Teaching and Contributes to Grade Inflation: A Theoretical and Empirical Analysis. www.tandfonline.com/doi/full/10.1080/01973533.2020.17568 17*	16
TechCrunch (2020). *https://techcrunch.com/2020/08/24/covid-19-pandemic-accelerated-shift-to-e-commerce-by-5-years-new-report-says*	3
Theall, M, and Franklin, J. (2002) *Looking for Bias in All the Wrong Places: A Search for Truth or a Witch Hunt in Student Ratings of Instruction? https://onlinelibrary.wiley.com/doi/abs/10.1002/*	16
Tse, H. (2021). *Plugged in But Disconnected: Challenges in the 2020 Online Transition.* Transitioning to Online Learning During Covid-19 Reflections by Practitioners. Edited by A. Hooke and G. Whateley. Sydney, Australia: Group Colleges Australia Pty Ltd, 95-99. ISBN 978-1-907453-30-4	8

Reference	Ch
Two-Sample T-Tests Allowing Unequal Variance. Retrieved from *https://ncss-wpengine.netdna-ssl.com/wp-content/themes/ncss/pdf/Procedures/PASS/Two-Sample_T-Tests_Allowing_Unequal_Variance*	9
Uddin, S. J. (2015). *Disengaged international students.* Negotiated Task submitted to Federation University for the partial fulfilment of Graduate Certificate in Higher Education qualification, 1-7.	8
Uddin, S. J. (2021). *Covid Driven Transition to Online Teaching: A Reflection. Transitioning to Online Learning During Covid-19 Reflections by Practitioners.* Edited by A. Hooke and G. Whateley. Sydney, Australia: Group Colleges Australia Pty Ltd, 43-48. ISBN 978-1-907453-30-4	8
UN Department of Economic and Social Affairs (2021). *The 17 Goals*, Retrieved from *https://sdgs.un.org/goals*	6
Vanderbilt (2021). *Student Evaluations of Teaching. https://www.vanderbilt.edu/course-teaching-evaluations/evaluation_reevaluation*	16
Varey, R., & Pirson, M. (Eds.). (2014). *Humanistic Marketing*. London, UK: Palgrave Macmillan.	2
Vowels, S. A., & Goldberg, K. L. (Eds.). (2019). *Teaching Data Analytics: Pedagogy and Program Design*. New York,: CRC Press.	1
West, A. (2021). What is meant by blended learning? Retrieved from *https://www.ubss.edu.au/media/2716/what-is-meant-by-blended-learning*	13
Whateley G. (2021) *Alternative Delivery Options*. Retrieved from *https://www.ubss.edu.au/articles/2021/september/alternative-delivery-options/*	11
Whateley, G. (2020) *Full marks for educators - the digital convicts of COVID-19*. Retrieved from *https://www.campusreview.com.au/2020/09/full-marks-for-educators-the-digital-convicts-of-covid-19/*	13

Reference	Ch
Whateley, G. (2021) *Understanding hybrid delivery*. Retrieved from	13
Whiting, K. (2020). *These are the top 10 skills of tomorrow*, World Economic Forum.	10
Wiig K. M. (1997) *Integrating Intellectual Capital and Knowledge Management*. Long Range Planning, Vol. 30, No. 3, pp. 399-405.	17
Wu, X., Kumar, V., Ross Quinlan, J., Ghosh, J., Yang, Q., Motoda, H., . Steinberg, D. (2007). *Top 10 algorithms in data mining. Knowledge and Information Systems*, 14(1), 1-37. doi:10.1007/s10115-007-0114-2.	1
Zepke, N., Leach, L. & Butler, P. (2014). *Student engagement: students' and teachers' perceptions*. Higher Education Research & Development, 33(2), 386-398.	8
Zhao, Y., Lin, S., Liu, J., Zhang, J., & Yu, Q. (2021). *Learning contextual factors, student engagement, and problem-solving skills: A Chinese perspective*. Social Behavior and Personality, 49(2), e 9796, https://doi.org/10.2224/sbp.9796, www.sbp-journal.com, 1-18.	8
Zuckerberg, M. (2021). *https://www.theverge.com/22588022/mark-zuckerberg-facebook-ceo-metaverse-interview*	3

List of Figures

List of Tables

About the Contributors

THE EDITORS

Angus Hooke

Is Emeritus Professor and Co-Director of the Centre for Scholarship and Research at UBSS. His earlier positions include Senior Economist at the IMF, Chief Economist at ABARE, Chief Economist at the NSW Treasury, Professor of Economics at Johns Hopkins University, and Director of the Entrepreneurship Department and Head of the Business School at the University of Nottingham, Ningbo, China. He has published 11 books and authored numerous academic journal articles.

Greg Whateley

Is Emeritus Professor and Deputy Vice Chancellor at Group Colleges Australia (GCA), and Executive Director of the GCA Board. Formerly, he was Chair of the Academic Board at the Australian Institute of Music and Dean of the College at Western Sydney University. In 2000, he co-invented 'The Virtual Conservatorium' and has since found himself involved in the development of the virtual school. He is a prolific author in academic journals and books and in industry journals.

THE FOREWORD

Alan Manly

Is a writer, company director and entrepreneur, with over 30 years' experience in the technology and education industries. Alan is a founding Director and Chief Executive Officer of the GCA Group of companies. He is a prolific author, having written two books and hundreds of articles. Alan was honoured in the Queen's Birthday 2021 Honours List with the Medal of the Order of Australia (OAM) in appreciation of his services to education.

THE AUTHORS

Mohammad Akbar

Is Assistant Professor at UBSS, lecturing in accounting subjects. He has MBAs from universities in both Bangladesh (Marketing) and Australia (Accounting). Mohammad is also Associate Dean (Learning and Teaching) at Polytechnic Institute of Australia, and a member of the Australian Integrity Committee. Currently he is pursuing research in accounting education at University Malaysia Perlis He has considerable professional experience in Marketing and Sales.

Sue Cameron

Is Assistant Professor at UBSS. She has won twice the UBSS Executive Dean's award for 'Outstanding Commitment to Teaching and Learning'. Prior to her academic career, Sue worked for 20-years at P&O Cruises, Australian Heritage Fleet, Australian Business Ltd and Outsource Australia in senior management positions covering HR, marketing, and operations. She has also established and managed four businesses, ranging from boat charters to property development.

Anurag Kanwar

Is Director of Compliance and Continuous Improvement at Group Colleges Australia (GCA), Executive Secretary of the GCA Board of Directors, and a member of the UBSS Academic Integrity Committee, Audit and Risk Committee, and Workplace Health and Safety Committee. Anurag is also a practicing lawyer in NSW, specialising in the areas of corporate governance and risk and is a Director of The Australian Risk Policy Institute (ARPI).

Harpreet Kaur

Is a Fellow of the Centre for Scholarship and Research (CSR) at UBSS. She has an MPHIL and a PhD in Economics. Harpreet teaches undergraduate and postgraduate courses at Charles Sturt University (CSU), Central Queensland University (CQU), and the Australian Institute of Higher education (AIH). Her research interests include the role of women in India and economic relationships between countries in Asia, Oceania, and the rest of the world.

Ajay Kumar

Is Assistant Professor at UBSS, lecturing in marketing management, organisational behaviour, project management and strategic management. Previously, he was Sessional Lead Lecturer at Central Queensland University. Ajay has professional experience as Business Development Manager and General Manager Marketing, Sales and Market Research. He is a member of several professional bodies and is NSW Emerging Marketing Mentor & Judge for AMI Awards.

Arash Najmaei

Holds a PhD in strategic management and entrepreneurship from Macquarie University. He is a marketing consultant but teaches part time at various universities. His teaching interests include business research methods, entrepreneurship, and media management. Arash's research has been published in journals and research books and presented at international conferences. He has received three best-paper awards for his research in entrepreneurship and research methods.

Nilima Paul

Is Assistant Professor in Accounting at UBSS. She has a Master of Commerce degree and a Doctor of Philosophy degree. Nilima is a member of the National Tax and Accounts Association, the Australian Institute of Training and Development, and the Association of Accounting Technicians. She teaches accounting subjects to undergraduate and postgraduate students in a range of universities and colleges and has won numerous awards for her commitment to teaching and learning.

Art Phillips

Is Adjunct Professor at UBSS and Director of the UBSS Centre for Entrepreneurship. He is a composer of film, television, and popular music and has worked in the film and television industries for over 30 years. Currently, he teaches in the MBA program at UBSS, adjudicates in the institution's undergraduate program and sits on several of its committees. He is passionate about keeping his lectures engaging for his students and has a profound interest in digital and virtual teaching.

Jotsana Roopram

Is Assistant Professor and Deputy Dean (Student Experience) at UBSS. Her main areas of expertise are examination management, developing academic systems, policy implementation in administrative processes and procedures, and school operations. Jotsana's research interests include governance and quality assurance in higher education, leadership, new managerialism, and online assessment. In 2021, Jotsana received the best chapter award in a book on scholarship.

Zahra Sadeghinejad

Is Assistant Professor at UBSS. She also teaches at Central Queensland University (CQU) and the International College of Management Sydney (ICMS). Zahra's main areas of teaching are marketing, media management, entrepreneurship, and quantitative methods. She has won several teaching awards. Zahra's research has been published as book chapters and journal articles and presented at international conferences, where she has received many best-paper awards.

Felix Stravens

Is Associate Professor, Deputy Dean - Academic, Program Director for the MBA degree, and Program Director for the Bachelor of Business degree at UBSS. He has 22 years of lecturing experience in the fields of marketing management, brand advertising strategies, and strategic marketing. His academic committee positions have included Chair of both the Academic Board at Queen Anne's School of Management and the Advertising Standards Authority of Singapore.

Harry Tse

Is Assistant Professor at UBSS and a Lecturer for the Economics Group, Business School, at the University of Technology, Sydney (UTS). Prior to joining the Business School at UTS, he was Head of the Economics & Statistics Department at UTS: Insearch. Harry has written two well-known textbooks on Economics (one published by Pearson and the other by McGraw-Hill) as well as 14 peer-reviewed journal articles and 11 conference papers.

Syed Uddin

Is Assistant Professor at UBSS where he lectures in business management, human resource management and organisational behaviour. Formerly, he was a Research Fellow at the Loughborough University Business School in the United Kingdom. Syed has written many refereed articles that have been published in prestigious academic journals. He is a six-time winner of the UBSS Executive Dean's award for 'Outstanding Commitment to Teaching and Learning'.

Andrew West

Is Dean of UBSS and Provost of the Blended Campus. Formerly, he was Director of the Centre for Entrepreneurship (CFE) at UBSS. Andrew has worked in academia for 14 years, following a successful 10-year career as an entrepreneur and business owner/manager. His research output includes 12 peer-reviewed journal articles and numerous conference papers. Andrew continues to carry out research in the areas of marketing and higher education.

Richard Xi

Is a Senior Postgraduate Coordinator and Assistant Professor at UBSS. His Australian education experience includes a Diploma of Business (SIT), a Diploma of Interpretation (NSIT), a Graduate Certificate in China Studies (USYD), a Graduate Certificate in Business Administration (UBSS), and a Master of Arts degree in Asian Studies (UNSW). He has been a keynote speaker in WSU's cross-cultural seminar program and a cultural adviser for two published books.

Notes pages

www.ingramcontent.com/pod-product-compliance
Lightning Source LLC
Chambersburg PA
CBHW070446100426
42812CB00004B/1220